Exercises to accompany

The Little, Brown
Essential Handbook

Seventh Edition

Jane E. Aaron

Longman

Boston   Columbus   Indianapolis   New York   San Francisco   Upper Saddle River
Amsterdam   Cape Town   Dubai   London   Madrid   Milan   Munich   Paris   Montreal   Toronto
Delhi   Mexico City   Sao Paulo   Sydney   Hong Kong   Seoul   Singapore   Taipei   Tokyo

Executive Editor: Suzanne Phelps Chambers
Senior Supplements Editor: Donna Campion
Electronic Page Makeup: Grapevine Publishing Services, Inc.

Exercises to accompany *The Little, Brown Essential Handbook,* Seventh Edition, by Jane E. Aaron.

1 2 3 4 5 6 7 8 9 10–OPM–13 12 11 10

Longman
is an imprint of

ISBN 13: 978-0-205-81742-9
ISBN 10:   0-205-81742-4

www.pearsonhighered.com

Preface

The seventy-one exercises in this book give students a chance to try out what they have learned from *The Little, Brown Essential Handbook,* Seventh Edition. The exercises range from editing for usage to correcting grammar and punctuation to working with sources and writing works-cited entries. With a few exceptions, all the work can be completed directly on the pages of the book. Like actual writing, the exercises are in connected discourse, with sentences building passages on cross-disciplinary topics such as literature, business practice, and animal behavior.

Each exercise is keyed directly to the relevant section(s) and page number(s) in *The Little, Brown Essential Handbook,* as in this sample exercise heading:

Exercise 10   REVISING: PARALLELISM
        Handbook Chapter 7, pp. 37–38

Students who have difficulty with any exercise should read the appropriate text explanation and then try again.

Almost all the exercises include one example illustrating what's required to complete the exercise. Then every exercise is accompanied by answers in the back of the book, an advantage for instructors discussing exercises with students or for students working independently.

Answers are labeled "possible" when the corresponding exercises encourage choice in responding and the given answers are but suggestions. Even for the objective exercises, which more often lend themselves to one response, some users may disagree with some answers. Usage is often flexible, and many rules allow interpretation. The answers here conform to the usage recommended in *The Little, Brown Essential Handbook.*

Contents

I. EFFECTIVE SENTENCES

II. GRAMMATICAL SENTENCES

Verbs

Pronouns

Modifiers

Sentence Faults

III. PUNCTUATION

IV. SPELLING AND MECHANICS

V. RESEARCH AND DOCUMENTATION

Effective Sentences

Exercise 1   R<small>EVISING</small>: E<small>MPHASIS OF SUBJECTS AND VERBS</small>
                    Handbook section 5a, p. 31

Rewrite the following sentences so that their subjects and verbs identify their key actors and actions.

Example:

The issue of students making a competition over grades is a reason why their focus on learning may be lost.

Students who compete over grades may lose their focus on learning.

1. The work of many heroes was crucial in helping to emancipate the slaves.

2. The contribution of Harriet Tubman, an escaped slave herself, included the guidance of hundreds of other slaves to freedom on the Underground Railroad.

3. A return to slavery was risked by Tubman or possibly death.

4. During the Civil War she was also a carrier of information from the South to the North.

5. After the war, needy former slaves were helped by Tubman's raising of money.

Exercise 2   SENTENCE COMBINING: EMPHASIS WITH BEGINNINGS
AND ENDINGS
Handbook section 5b, p. 32

Locate the main idea in each group of sentences below. Then combine each group into a single sentence that emphasizes that idea by placing it at the beginning or the end. For sentences 2–5, determine the position of the main idea by considering its relation to the previous sentences: if the main idea picks up a topic that has already been introduced, place it at the beginning; if it adds new information, place it at the end.

Example:

The storm blew roofs off buildings. It caused extensive damage. It knocked down many trees. It severed power lines.

Main idea at beginning: The storm caused extensive damage, blowing roofs off buildings, knocking down many trees, and severing power lines.

Main idea at end: Blowing roofs off buildings, knocking down many trees, and severing power lines, the storm caused extensive damage.

1. Pat Taylor strode into the room. The room was packed. He greeted students called "Taylor's Kids." He nodded to their parents and teachers.

2. This was a wealthy Louisiana oilman. He had promised his "Kids" free college educations. He was determined to make higher education available to all qualified but disadvantaged students.

3. The students welcomed Taylor. Their voices joined in singing. They sang "You Are the Wind Beneath My Wings." Their faces beamed with hope. Their eyes flashed with self-confidence.

4. The students had thought a college education was beyond their dreams. It seemed too costly. It seemed too demanding.

5. Taylor had to ease the costs and the demands of getting to college. He created a bold plan. The plan consisted of scholarships, tutoring, and counseling.

Exercise 3   SENTENCE COMBINING: COORDINATION
Handbook section 5c, p. 33

Combine sentences in the following passages to coordinate related ideas in the way that seems most effective to you. You will have to supply coordinating conjunctions or conjunctive adverbs and the appropriate punctuation.

1. Many chronic misspellers do not have the time to master spelling rules. They may not have the motivation. They rely on dictionaries to catch misspellings. Most dictionaries list words under their correct spellings. One kind of dictionary is designed for chronic misspellers. It lists each word under its common *mis*spellings. It then provides the correct spelling. It also provides the definition.

2. Henry Hudson was an English explorer. He captained ships for the Dutch East India Company. On a voyage in 1610 he passed by Greenland. He sailed into a great bay in today's northern Canada. He thought he and his sailors could winter there. The cold was terrible. Food ran out. The sailors mutinied. The sailors cast Hudson adrift in a small boat. Eight others were also in the boat. Hudson and his companions perished.

Exercise 4 SENTENCE COMBINING: SUBORDINATION
Handbook section 5d, p. 34

Combine each of the following pairs of sentences twice, each time using one of the subordinate structures in parentheses to make a single sentence. You will have to add, delete, change, and rearrange words.

Example:

During the late eighteenth century, workers carried beverages in brightly colored bottles. The bottles had cork stoppers. (*Clause beginning that. Phrase beginning with.*)

During the late eighteenth century, workers carried beverages in brightly colored bottles that had cork stoppers.

During the late eighteenth century, workers carried beverages in brightly colored bottles with cork stoppers.

1. The bombardier beetle sees an enemy. It shoots out a jet of chemicals to protect itself. (*Clause beginning when. Phrase beginning seeing.*)

2. The beetle's spray is very potent. It consists of hot and irritating chemicals. (*Phrase beginning consisting. Phrase beginning of.*)

3. The spray is a most dangerous weapon against enemies. It is harmless to the beetle. (*Clause beginning although. Appositive beginning a most.*)

4. The beetle's spray is a series of tiny chemical explosions. The spray is discharged as a pulsed jet. (*Phrase beginning discharged. Appositive beginning a series.*)

5. Scientists filmed the beetle. They discovered that this jet pulses five hundred times each second. (*Clause beginning who. Phrase beginning filming.*)

6. The jet's two chemicals are stored separately in the beetle's body and mixed in the spraying gland. The chemicals resemble a nerve-gas weapon. (*Phrase beginning stored. Clause beginning which.*)

7. The tip of the beetle's abdomen sprays the chemicals. The tip revolves like a turret on a World War II bomber. *(Phrase beginning revolving. Phrase beginning spraying.)*

8. The spray is accompanied by a popping sound. It travels twenty-six miles per hour. (*Phrase beginning accompanied. Clause beginning which.*)

9. The beetle is less than an inch long. It has many enemies. (*Clause beginning because. Phrase beginning less.*)

10. The beetle defeats most of its enemies. It is still eaten by spiders and birds. (*Clause beginning although. Phrase beginning except.*)

Exercise 5   REVISING: COORDINATION AND SUBORDINATION
Handbook sections 5c–5d, pp. 33–34

The following paragraph consists entirely of simple sentences. Use coordination and subordination to combine sentences in the way you think most effective to emphasize main ideas.

Sir Walter Raleigh personified the Elizabethan Age. That was the period of Elizabeth I's rule of England. The period occurred in the last half of the sixteenth century. Raleigh was a courtier and poet. He was also an explorer and entrepreneur. Supposedly, he gained Queen Elizabeth's favor. He did this by throwing his cloak beneath her feet at the right moment. She was just about to step over a puddle. There is no evidence for this story. It does illustrate Raleigh's dramatic and dynamic personality. His energy drew others to him. He was one of Elizabeth's favorites. She supported him. She also dispensed favors to him. However, he lost his queen's goodwill. Without her permission he seduced one of her maids of honor. He eventually married the maid of honor. Elizabeth died. Then her successor imprisoned Raleigh in the Tower of London. Her successor was James I. The king falsely charged Raleigh with treason. Raleigh was released after thirteen years. He was arrested again two years later on the old treason charges. At the age of sixty-six he was beheaded.

Exercise 6   REVISING: EMPTY WORDS AND PHRASES
Handbook section 6b, p. 35

Revise the following sentences to achieve conciseness by cutting filler phrases, qualifying phrases, and all-purpose words.

Example:

I came to college because of many factors, but most of all because of the fact that I want a career in medicine.

I came to college mainly because I want a career in medicine.

1. *Gerrymandering* refers to a situation in which the lines of a voting district are redrawn to benefit a particular party or ethnic group.

2. The name is explained by the fact that Elbridge Gerry, the governor of Massachusetts in 1812, redrew voting districts in Essex County.

3. On the map one new district looked in the nature of a salamander.

4. Upon seeing the map, a man who was for all intents and purposes a critic of Governor Gerry's administration cried out, "Gerrymander!"

5. At the present time, a dominant political group may try to change the character of a district's voting pattern by gerrymandering to exclude rival groups' supporters.

Exercise 7   REVISING: UNNECESSARY REPETITION
Handbook section 6c, p. 36

Revise the following sentences to achieve conciseness. Concentrate on eliminating repetition and redundancy.

Example:

Because the circumstances surrounding the cancellation of classes were murky and unclear, the editor of the student newspaper assigned a staff reporter to investigate and file a report on the circumstances.

Because the circumstances leading to the cancellation of classes were unclear, the editor of the student newspaper assigned a staffer to investigate and report the story.

1. Some Vietnam veterans coming back to the United States after their tours of duty in Vietnam had problems readjusting again to life in America.

2. Afflicted with post-traumatic stress disorder, a psychological disorder that sometimes arises after a trauma, some of the veterans had psychological problems that caused them to have trouble holding jobs and maintaining relationships.

3. Some who used to use drugs in Vietnam could not break their drug habits after they returned back to the United States.

4. The few veterans who committed crimes and violent acts gained so much notoriety and fame that many Americans thought all veterans were crazy, insane maniacs.

5. As a result of such stereotyping of Vietnam-era veterans, veterans are included into the same antidiscrimination laws that protect other victims of discrimination.

Exercise 8   REVISING: CONCISENESS
Handbook sections 6d–6f, pp. 36–37

Rewrite each passage below into a single concise sentence. As necessary, combine sentences, reduce grammatical structures, replace weak verbs with strong ones, and eliminate passive and expletive constructions.

Example:

He was taking some exercise in the park. Then several thugs were suddenly ahead in his path.

He was exercising [or jogging or strolling] in the park when several thugs suddenly loomed in his path.

1. Chewing gum was originally introduced to the United States by Antonio López de Santa Anna. He was the Mexican general.

2. After he had been defeated by the Texans in 1854, the general, who was exiled, made the choice to settle in New York.

3. A piece of chicle had been stashed by the general in his baggage. Chicle is the dried milky sap of the Mexican sapodilla tree.

4. There was more of this resin brought into the country by Santa Anna's friend Thomas Adams. Adams had a plan to make rubber.

5. The plan failed. Then Adams had occasion to get a much more successful idea on the basis of the use to which the resin was put by
General Santa Anna. That is, Adams decided to make a gum that
could be chewed.

Exercise 9   **REVISING: CONCISENESS**
Handbook Chapter 6, pp. 34–37

Make the following paragraph as concise as possible. Cut unneeded or re-
peated words, and simplify words and grammatical structures. Consult a
dictionary as needed. Be merciless.

Example:

The nursery school teacher education training sessions involve active
interfacing with preschool children of the appropriate age as well as
intensive peer interaction in the form of role plays.

Training for nursery school teachers involves interaction with preschoolers
and role playing with peers.

At the end of a lengthy line of reasoning, he came to the conclusion

that the situation with carcinogens [cancer-causing substances] should be

regarded as similar to the situation with the automobile. Instead of giving

in to an irrational fear of cancer, we should consider all aspects of the prob-

lem in a balanced and dispassionate frame of mind, making a total of the

benefits received from potential carcinogens (plastics, pesticides, and other

similar products) and measuring said total against the damage done by such products. This is the nature of most discussions about the automobile. Instead of responding irrationally to the visual, aural, and air pollution caused by automobiles, we have decided to live with them (while simultaneously working to improve on them) for the benefits brought to society as a whole.

Exercise 10   REVISING: PARALLELISM
                   Handbook Chapter 7, pp. 37–38

Revise the following sentences to create parallelism wherever it is required for grammar and coherence. Add or delete words or rephrase as necessary.

Example:

After emptying her bag, searching the apartment, and she called the library, Jennifer realized she had lost the book.

After emptying her bag, searching the apartment, and calling the library, Jennifer realized she had lost the book.

1. The ancient Greeks celebrated four athletic contests: the Olympic Games at Olympia, the Isthmian Games were held near Corinth, at Delphi the Pythian Games, and the Nemean Games were sponsored by the people of Cleonae.

2. Each day the games consisted of either athletic events or holding ceremonies and sacrifices to the gods.

3. In the years between the games, competitors were taught wrestling, javelin throwing, and how to box.

4. Competitors participated in running sprints, spectacular chariot and horse races, and running long distances while wearing full armor.

5. The purpose of such events was developing physical strength, demonstrating skill and endurance, and to sharpen the skills needed for war.

6. Events were held for both men and for boys.

7. At the Olympic Games the spectators cheered their favorites to victory, attended sacrifices to the gods, and they feasted on the meat not burned in offerings.

8. The athletes competed less to achieve great wealth than for gaining honor both for themselves and their cities.

9. Of course, exceptional athletes received financial support from patrons, poems and statues by admiring artists, and they even got lavish living quarters from their sponsoring cities.

10. With the medal counts and flag ceremonies, today's Olympians sometimes seem to be proving their countries' superiority more than to demonstrate individual talent.

Exercise 11   SENTENCE COMBINING: PARALLELISM
Handbook Chapter 7, pp. 37–38

Combine each group of sentences below into one concise sentence in which parallel elements appear in parallel structures. You will have to add, delete, change, and rearrange words. Each item has more than one possible answer.

Example:

The new process works smoothly. It is efficient, too.

The new process works smoothly and efficiently.

1. People can develop post-traumatic stress disorder (PTSD). They develop it after experiencing a dangerous situation. They will also have felt fear for their survival.

2. The disorder can be triggered by a wide variety of events. Combat is a typical cause. Similarly, natural disasters can result in PTSD. Some people experience PTSD after a hostage situation.

3. PTSD can occur immediately after the stressful incident. Or it may not appear until many years later.

4. Sometimes people with PTSD will act irrationally. Moreover, they often become angry.

5. Other symptoms include dreaming that one is reliving the experience. They include hallucinating that one is back in the terrifying place. In another symptom one imagines that strangers are actually one's former torturers.

6. Victims of the disorder might isolate themselves from family and friends. They can stop going to work. Criminal acts might be committed. Or doing violence to themselves or others is a possibility.

7. Victims might need private counseling. Some might need to be hospitalized.

8. The healing process is terrifying when the patients begin. But it becomes exciting when they improve.

9. After treatment many patients overcome their fears. And they seldom experience any recurrence of the symptoms.

10. Victims learn the roots of their fears. Then they are relieved of their pain. Usually they are restored to their families. And they return to a productive place in society.

Exercise 12   REVISING: VARIETY
Handbook section 8a, p. 39

The following paragraph consists entirely of simple sentences that begin with their subjects. As appropriate, vary sentences so that the paragraph is more readable and its important ideas stand out clearly. You will have to delete, add, change, and rearrange words.

The Italian volcano Vesuvius had been dormant for many years. It then exploded on August 24 in the year AD 79. The ash, pumice, and mud from the volcano buried two busy towns. Herculaneum is one. The more famous is Pompeii. Both towns lay undiscovered for many centuries. Herculaneum and Pompeii were discovered in 1709 and 1748, respectively. The excavation of Pompeii was the more systematic. It was the occasion for initiating modern methods of conservation and restoration. Herculaneum was simply looted of its more valuable finds. It was then left to disintegrate. Pompeii appears much as it did before the eruption. A luxurious house opens onto a lush central garden. An election poster decorates a wall. A dining table is set for breakfast.

Exercise 13   REVISING: APPROPRIATE WORDS
Handbook Chapter 9, pp. 41–46

Rewrite the following sentences as needed for standard American English. Consult a dictionary to determine whether particular words are appropriate and to find suitable substitutes.

Example:

If negotiators get hyper during contract discussions, they may mess up chances for a settlement.

If negotiators become excited or upset during contract discussions, they may harm chances for a settlement.

1. Acquired Immune Deficiency Syndrome (AIDS) is a major deal all

   over the world.

2. The disease gets around primarily by sexual intercourse, exchange of

   bodily fluids, shared needles, and blood transfusions.

3. Those who think the disease is limited to homos, druggies, and for-

   eigners are quite mistaken.

4. Stats suggest that in the United States one in every five hundred college

   kids carries the HIV virus that causes AIDS.

5. A person with HIV or full-blown AIDS does not deserve to be subject-

   ed to exclusionary behavior or callousness on the part of his fellow cit-

   izens. Instead, he has the necessity for all the compassion, medical care,

   and financial assistance due those who are in the extremity of illness.

6. An HIV or AIDS victim often sees a team of doctors or a single doctor with a specialized practice.

7. The doctor may help his patients by obtaining social services for them as well as by providing medical care.

8. The HIV or AIDS sufferer who loses his job may need public assistance.

9. For someone who is very ill, a home-care nurse may be necessary. She can administer medications and make the sick person as comfortable as possible.

10. Some people with HIV or AIDS have insurance, but others lack the dough for premiums.

Exercise 14   REVISING: EXACT WORDS
Handbook Chapter 10, pp. 46–48

Revise the following sentences to replace any underlined word that is used incorrectly. Consult a dictionary if you are uncertain of a word's precise meaning.

Example:

Sam and Dave are going to Bermuda and Hauppauge, <u>respectfully,</u> for spring vacation.

Sam and Dave are going to Bermuda and Hauppauge, <u>respectively,</u> for spring vacation.

1. Maxine Hong Kingston was <u>rewarded</u> many prizes for her first two books, *The Woman Warrior* and *China Men.*

2. Kingston <u>sites</u> her mother's tales about ancestors and ancient Chinese customs as the sources of these memoirs.

3. Two of Kingston's <u>progeny</u>, her great-grandfathers, are focal points of *China Men.*

4. Both men led rebellions against <u>suppressive</u> employers: a sugarcane farmer and a railroad-construction supervisor.

5. In her childhood Kingston was greatly <u>effected</u> by her mother's tale about a pregnant aunt who was <u>ostracized</u> by villagers.

6. The aunt gained <u>avengeance</u> by drowning herself in the village's water supply.

7. Kingston decided to make her nameless relative <u>infamous</u> by giving her <u>immortality</u> in *The Woman Warrior.*

8. Kingston's novel *Tripmaster Monkey* has been called the <u>premier</u> novel about the 1960s.

9. Her characters <u>embody</u> the <u>principles</u> that led her to her own protest against the Vietnam War.

10. Kingston's innovative books <u>infer</u> her opposition to racism and sexism both in the China of the past and in the United States of the present.

Exercise 15   **REVISING: CONCRETE AND SPECIFIC WORDS**
Handbook section 10b, p. 47

Make the following paragraph vivid by expanding the sentences with appropriate details of your own choosing. Concentrate especially on substituting concrete and specific words for the abstract and general ones that are underlined.

Example:

The <u>long</u> flood caused a lot of <u>awful</u> destruction in the town.

The flood waters, which rose swiftly and then stayed stubbornly high for days, killed at least six townspeople and made life a misery for the hundreds who had to evacuate their ruined homes and stores.

I remember <u>clearly</u> how <u>awful</u> I felt the first time I <u>attended</u> Mrs. Murphy's second-grade class. I had <u>recently</u> moved from a <u>small</u> town in Missouri to a <u>crowded</u> suburb of Chicago. My new school looked <u>big</u> from the outside and seemed <u>dark</u> inside as I <u>walked</u> down the <u>long</u> corridor toward the classroom. The class was <u>noisy</u> as I neared the door; but when I <u>entered</u>, <u>everyone</u> became <u>quiet</u> and <u>looked</u> at me. I felt <u>uncomfortable</u> and <u>wanted</u> a place to hide. However, in a <u>loud</u> voice Mrs. Murphy <u>directed</u> me to the front of the room to introduce myself.

Exercise 16   USING PREPOSITIONS IN IDIOMS
Handbook section 10c, p. 47

Insert the preposition that correctly completes each idiom in the following sentences.

Example:

I disagree _____ many feminists who say women should not be homemakers.

I disagree <u>with</u> many feminists who say women should not be homemakers.

1. Children are waiting longer to become independent _____ their parents.

2. According _____ US Census data for young adults ages eighteen to twenty-four, 57 percent of men and 47 percent of women live full-time with their parents.

3. Some of these adult children are dependent _____ their parents financially.

4. In other cases, the parents charge their children _____ housing, food, and other living expenses.

5. Many adult children are financially capable _____ living independently but prefer to save money rather than contend _____ high housing costs.

Exercise 17   REVISING: CLICHÉS
Handbook section 10d, p. 47

Revise the following sentences to eliminate trite expressions.

Example:

The basketball team had almost seized victory, but it faced the test of truth in the last quarter of the game.

The basketball team <u>seemed about to win</u>, but the <u>real test</u> came in the last quarter of the game.

1. Our reliance on foreign oil to support our driving habit has hit record highs in recent years.

2. Gas-guzzling vehicles are responsible for part of the increase.

3. In the future, we may have to bite the bullet and use public transportation or drive only fuel-efficient cars.

4. Both solutions are easier said than done.

5. But it stands to reason that we cannot go on using the world's oil reserves at such a rapid rate.

II
Grammatical Sentences

VERBS

Exercise 18   USING IRREGULAR VERBS
Handbook section 11a, p. 51

For each irregular verb in brackets, supply either the past tense or the past participle, as appropriate, and identify the form you used.

Example:

Though we had [hide] the cash box, it was [steal].

Though we had <u>hidden</u> the cash box, it was <u>stolen</u>. [Two past participles.]

1. The world population has [grow] by two-thirds of a billion people in less than a decade.

2. Recently it [break] the 6 billion mark.

3. Experts have [draw] pictures of a crowded future.

4. They predict that the world population may have [slide] up to as much as 10 billion by the year 2050.

5. Though the food supply [rise] in the last decade, the share to each person [fall].

6. At the same time the water supply, which had actually [become] healthier in the twentieth century, [sink] in size and quality.

7. The number of species on earth [shrink] by 20 percent.

8. Changes in land use [run] nomads and subsistence farmers off the land.

9. Yet all has not been [lose].

10. Recently human beings have [begin] to heed these and other problems and to explore how technology can be [drive] to help the earth and all its populations.

Exercise 19   COMBINING HELPING VERBS AND MAIN VERBS (ESL)
                    Handbook section 11b, p. 51

Revise the following sentences so that helping verbs and main verbs are used correctly. If a sentence is correct as given, circle the number preceding it.

Example:

The college testing service has test as many as five hundred students at one time.

The college testing service has <u>tested</u> as many as five hundred students at one time.

1. A report from the Bureau of the Census has confirm a widening gap between rich and poor.

2. As suspected, the percentage of people below the poverty level did increased over the last decade.

3. More than 17 percent of the population is make 5 percent of all the income.

4. About 1 percent of the population will keeping an average of $500,000 apiece after taxes.

5. The other 99 percent all together will retain about $300,000.

6. More than 80 percent of American families will may make less than $65,000 per family this year.

7. Fewer than 5 percent of families could to make more than $110,000 per family.

8. At the same time that the gap is widen, many people are work longer hours.

9. Many workers once might have change jobs to increase their pay.

10. Now these workers are remain with the jobs they have.

Exercise 20   **REVISING: VERBS PLUS GERUNDS OR INFINITIVES (ESL)**
Handbook section 11c, p. 54

Revise the following sentences so that gerunds or infinitives are used correctly with verbs. If a sentence is correct as given, circle the number preceding it.

Example:

A politician cannot avoid to alienate some voters.

A politician cannot avoid <u>alienating</u> some voters.

1. A program called HELP Wanted tries to encourage citizens take action on behalf of American competitiveness.

2. Officials working on this program hope improving education for work.

3. One statistic that makes the government worry is the high rate of illiteracy in the United States.

4. American businesses find that some workers need learning to read.

5. In fact, many US companies have their workers to attend classes.

6. New York Life Insurance Company quit to process claims in the US because of illiteracy among workers.

7. Motorola requires applicants taking an exam in math.

8. In the next ten years the United States expects facing a shortage of 350,000 scientists.

9. HELP Wanted suggests creating a media campaign.

10. It hopes to expose the vital relationships among education, jobs, and economic progress.

Exercise 21   REVISING: VERBS PLUS PARTICLES (ESL)
Handbook section 11d, p. 55

The two- and three-word verbs in the sentences below are underlined. Some are correct as given, and some are not because they should or should not be separated by other words. Revise the verbs and other words that are incorrect.

Example:

Hollywood producers never seem to come up with entirely new plots, but they also never run new ways out of to present old ones.

Hollywood producers never seem to come up with [*correct*] entirely new plots, but they also never run out of new ways to present old ones.

1. American movies treat everything from going out with someone to making up an ethnic identity, but few people look their significance into.

2. While some viewers <u>stay away from</u> topical films, others <u>turn</u> at the theater <u>up</u> simply because a movie has sparked debate.

3. Some movies attracted rowdy viewers, and the theaters had to <u>throw</u> <u>out</u> them.

4. Filmmakers have always been eager to <u>point</u> their influence <u>out</u> to the public.

5. Everyone agrees that filmmakers will <u>keep</u> creating controversy <u>on</u>, if only because it can <u>fill up</u> theaters.

Exercise 22   ADJUSTING TENSE SEQUENCE: PAST OR PAST PERFECT TENSE
Handbook section 12d, p. 57

The tenses in each sentence below are in correct sequence. Change the tense of one verb as instructed. Then change the tenses of other verbs as needed to restore correct sequence. Some items have more than one possible answer.

Example:

Delgado will call when he reaches his destination. (*Change <u>will call to</u>* <u>*called*</u>.)

Delgado called when he <u>reached</u> [*or* had reached] his destination.

1. Diaries that Adolf Hitler is supposed to have written have surfaced in Germany. (*Change <u>have surfaced to</u> <u>had surfaced</u>*.)

2. Many people believe that the diaries are authentic because a well-known historian has declared them so. (*Change believe to believed.*)

3. However, the historian's evaluation has been questioned by other authorities, who call the diaries forgeries. (*Change has been questioned to was questioned.*)

4. They claim, among other things, that the paper is not old enough to have been used by Hitler. (*Change claim to claimed.*)

5. Eventually, the doubters will win the debate because they have the best evidence. (*Change will win to won.*)

Exercise 23   **REVISING: CONSISTENCY IN TENSE AND MOOD**
Handbook sections 12c, 13b; pp. 56, 58

Revise the following sentences to make them consistent in tense and mood.

Example:

Lynn ran to first, rounded the base, and keeps running until she slides into second.

Lynn ran to first, rounded the base, and kept running until she slid into second.

1. When your cholesterol count is too high, adjusting your diet and exercise level reduced it.

2. After you lowered your cholesterol rate, you decrease the chances of heart attack and stroke.

3. First eliminate saturated fats from your diet; then you should consume more whole grains and raw vegetables.

4. To avoid saturated fats, substitute turkey and chicken for beef, and you should use cholesterol-free margarine, salad dressing, and cooking oil.

5. A regular program of aerobic exercise, such as walking or swimming, improves your cholesterol rate and made you feel much healthier.

Exercise 24   REVISING: SUBJUNCTIVE MOOD
Handbook section 13a, p. 58

Revise the following sentences with appropriate subjunctive verb forms.

Example:

I would exercise if I wasn't so busy.

I would exercise if I weren't so busy.

1. If John Hawkins would have known of all the dangerous side effects of smoking tobacco, would he have introduced the dried plant to England in 1565?

2. Hawkins noted that if a Florida Indian man was to travel for several days, he would have smoked tobacco to satisfy his hunger and thirst.

3. Early tobacco growers feared that their product would not gain acceptance unless it was perceived as healthful.

4. To prevent fires, in 1646 the General Court of Massachusetts passed a law requiring that colonists smoked tobacco only if they were five miles from any town.

5. To prevent decadence, in 1647 Connecticut passed a law mandating that one's smoking of tobacco was limited to once a day in one's own home.

Exercise 25   CONVERTING BETWEEN ACTIVE AND PASSIVE VOICES
Handbook section 14a, p. 59

To practice using the two voices of the verb, convert the verbs in the following sentences from active to passive or from passive to active. (In converting from passive to active, you may have to add a subject.) Which version of each sentence seems more effective? Why?

Example:

The aspiring actor was discovered in a nightclub.

A talent scout discovered the aspiring actor in a nightclub.

1. When the Eiffel Tower was built in 1889, it was thought by the French to be ugly.

2. At the time, many people still resisted industrial technology.

3. The tower's naked steel construction typified this technology.

4. Beautiful ornament was expected to grace fine buildings.

5. Further, a structure without solid walls could not even be called a building.

Exercise 26   REVISING: CONSISTENCY IN SUBJECT AND VOICE
Handbook section 14b, p. 60

Make the following sentences consistent in subject and voice.

Example:

At the reunion they ate hot dogs and volleyball was played.

At the reunion they ate hot dogs and played volleyball.

1. If students learn how to study efficiently, much better grades will be

   made on tests.

2. Conscientious students begin to prepare for tests immediately after

   the first class is attended.

3. Before each class all reading assignments are completed, and the stu-

   dents answer any study questions.

4. In class they listen carefully and good notes are taken.

5. Questions are asked by the students when they do not understand

   the instructor.

Exercise 27   REVISING: SUBJECT-VERB AGREEMENT
Handbook Chapter 15, pp. 60–63

Revise the verbs in the following sentences as needed to make subjects and verbs agree in number. If the sentence is correct as given, circle the number preceding it.

Example:

Each of the job applicants type sixty words per minute.

Each of the job applicants <u>types</u> sixty words per minute.

1. Weinstein & Associates are a consulting firm that try to make busi-

   nesspeople laugh.

2. Statistics from recent research suggests that humor relieves stress.

3. Reduced stress in businesses in turn reduce illness and absenteeism.

4. Reduced stress can also reduce friction within an employee group,

   which then work together more productively.

5. In special conferences held by one consultant, each of the participants

   practice making others laugh.

6. "Isn't there enough laughs within you to spread the wealth?" the consultant asks his students.

7. The consultant quotes Casey Stengel's rule that the best way to keep your management job is to separate the underlings who hate you from the ones who have not decided how they feel.

8. Such self-deprecating comments in public is uncommon among business managers, the consultant says.

9. Each of the managers in a typical firm take the work much too seriously.

10. The humorous boss often feels like the only one of the managers who have other things in mind besides profits.

11. One consultant to many companies suggest cultivating office humor with practical jokes such as a rubber fish in the water cooler.

12. When a manager or employees regularly posts cartoons on the bulletin board, office spirit usually picks up.

13. When someone who has seemed too easily distracted is entrusted with updating the cartoons, his or her concentration often improves.

14. In the face of levity, the former sourpuss becomes one of those who

hides bad temper.

15. Every one of the consultants caution, however, that humor has no

place in life-affecting corporate situations such as employee layoffs.

PRONOUNS

Exercise 28   CHOOSING SUBJECTIVE OR OBJECTIVE PRONOUNS:
SUBJECTS, OBJECTS, SUBJECT COMPLEMENTS
Handbook sections 16a–16b, pp. 63–64

From the pairs in brackets, select the appropriate subjective or objective
pronoun(s) for each of the following sentences.

Example:

"Between you and [I, me]," the seller said, "this deal is a steal."

"Between you and me," the seller said, "this deal is a steal."

1. Jody and [I, me] had been hunting for jobs.

2. The best employees at our old company were [she, her] and [I, me],
so [we, us] expected to find jobs quickly.

3. One company did offer jobs to both [she, her] and [I, me].

4. After [she, her] and [I, me] had discussed the offers with several people, however, [we, us] both decided to decline.

5. The jobs did not seem appropriate for [we, us] if [we, us] wanted to
become management trainees.

6. That left [she, her] with only one offer and [I, me] with none.

7. Between [she, her] and [I, me] the job search had lasted two months, and still it had barely begun.

8. Slowly, [she, her] and [I, me] stopped sharing leads.

9. It was obvious that Jody and [I, me] could not be as friendly as [we, us] had been.

10. Sadly, money seemed to mean more to [she, her] and [I, me] than our friendship.

Exercise 29   CHOOSING BETWEEN *WHO* AND *WHOM*
            Handbook section 16c, p. 64

From the pairs in brackets, select the appropriate form of the pronoun in each of the following sentences.

Example:

My mother asked me [who, whom] I was meeting.

My mother asked me whom I was meeting.

1. The school administrators suspended Jurgen, [who, whom] they suspected of setting the fire.

2. Jurgen had been complaining to other custodians, [who, whom] reported him.

3. He constantly complained of unfair treatment from [whoever, whomever] happened to be passing in the halls, including pupils.

4. "[Who, Whom] here has heard Mr. Jurgen's complaints?" the police asked.

5. "[Who, Whom] did he complain most about?"

6. His coworkers agreed that Jurgen seemed less upset with the staff or students, most of [who, whom] he did not even know, than with the building itself.

7. "He took out his aggression on the building," claimed one coworker [who, whom] often witnessed Jurgen's behavior.

8. "He cursed and kicked the walls and [whoever, whomever] he saw nearby."

9. The coworker thought that Jurgen might have imagined people [who, whom] instructed him to behave the way he did.

10. "He's someone [who, whom] other people can't get next to," said the coworker.

Exercise 30   REVISING: PRONOUN FORMS
Handbook Chapter 16, pp. 63–66

Revise all inappropriate case forms in the following sentences. If a sentence is correct as given, circle the number preceding it.

Example:

Convincing we veterans to vote yes will be difficult.

Convincing us veterans to vote yes will be difficult.

1. Written four thousand years ago, *The Epic of Gilgamesh* tells of a bored king who his people thought was too harsh.

2. Gilgamesh found a source of entertainment when he met Enkidu, a wild man who had lived with the animals in the mountains.

3. Him and Gilgamesh wrestled to see whom was more powerful.

4. After hours of struggle, Enkidu admitted that Gilgamesh was stronger than he.

5. The friendship of the two strong men was sealed by them fighting.

6. Gilgamesh said, "Between you and I, mighty deeds will be accomplished, and our fame will be everlasting."

7. Among their glorious acts, Enkidu and him defeated a giant bull, Humbaba, and cut down the bull's cedar forests.

8. Their bringing back cedar logs to Gilgamesh's treeless land won great praise from the people.

9. When Enkidu died, Gilgamesh mourned his death, realizing that no one had been a better friend than him.

10. When Gilgamesh himself died many years later, his people raised a

monument praising Enkidu and he for their friendship and their

mighty deeds of courage.

Exercise 31   REVISING: PRONOUN-ANTECEDENT AGREEMENT
Handbook Chapter 17, pp. 66–67

Revise the following sentences so that pronouns and their antecedents agree
in person and number. Some items have more than one possible answer.
Try to avoid the generic *he*. If you change the subject of a sentence, be sure
to change the verb as necessary for agreement. If the sentence is correct as
given, circle the number preceding it.

Example:

Each of the Boudreaus' children brought their laundry home at
Thanksgiving.

Each of the Boudreaus' children brought laundry home at Thanksgiving. Or:
All of the Boudreaus' children brought their laundry home at Thanksgiving.
Or: Each of the Boudreaus' children brought his or her laundry home at
Thanksgiving.

1. Each girl raised in a Mexican American family in the Rio Grande

Valley of Texas hopes that one day they will be given a *quinceañera*

party for their fifteenth birthday.

2. Such celebrations are very expensive because it entails a religious ser-

vice followed by a huge party.

3. A girl's immediate family, unless they are wealthy, cannot afford the

    party by themselves.

4. The parents will ask each close friend or relative if they can help with

    the preparations.

5. Surrounded by her family and attended by her friends and their

    escorts, the *quinceañera* is introduced as a young woman eligible for

    Mexican American society.

Exercise 32   **REVISING: UNCLEAR PRONOUN REFERENCE**
Handbook Chapter 18, pp. 68–70

Rewrite the following sentences to eliminate unclear pronoun reference. If
you use a pronoun in your revision, be sure that it refers to only one
antecedent and that it falls close enough to its antecedent to ensure clarity.

Example:

Saul found an old gun in the rotting shed that was just as his grandfather had left it.

In the rotting shed Saul found an old gun that was just as his grandfather
had left it.

1. There is a difference between the heroes of the twentieth century and
   the heroes of earlier times: they have flaws in their characters.

2. Sports fans still admire Pete Rose, Babe Ruth, and Joe Namath even
   though they could not be perfect.

3. Fans liked Rose for having his young son serve as bat boy when he was in Cincinnati.

4. Rose's reputation as a gambler and tax evader may overshadow his reputation as a ballplayer, but it will survive.

5. Rose amassed an unequaled record as a hitter, using his bat to do things no one else has ever done. It stands even though Rose was banned from baseball.

6. Fans knew about Babe Ruth's drinking and carousing, but it did not stop them from cheering him.

7. Fans were happy if Ruth hit home runs and won games, and the Yankee owners wanted to fill the stadium. "The Bambino" seldom failed to satisfy them.

8. With his bat Ruth achieved the record for most home runs in a career. Nearly half a century passed before Henry Aaron broke it.

9. When he was quarterback of the New York Jets, a reporter was told by Joe Namath that he would have to quit football because he was part-owner of a restaurant that mobsters supposedly also owned.

10. Choosing between restaurant and career, Namath sold it.

Exercise 33   REVISING: SPECIFIC ANTECEDENTS
Handbook section 18c, p. 68

Many of the pronouns in the following sentences do not refer to specific, appropriate antecedents. Revise the sentences as necessary to make them clear.

Example:

In Grand Teton National Park they have moose, elk, and trumpeter swans.

Moose, elk, and trumpeter swans live in Grand Teton National Park.

1. "Life begins at forty" is a cliché many people live by, and this may or may not be true.

2. When she was forty, Pearl Buck's novel *The Good Earth* won the Pulitzer Prize.

3. In *The Good Earth* you have to struggle, but fortitude is rewarded.

4. In the British House of Commons they did not welcome forty-year-old Nancy Astor as the first female member when she entered in 1919.

5. In AD 610 Muhammad, age forty, began to have a series of visions that became the foundation of the Muslim faith. Since then, millions of people have become one.

Exercise 34   REVISING: CONSISTENCY IN PRONOUNS AND ANTECEDENTS
Handbook section 18d, p. 69

Revise the following sentences to make them consistent in person and number.

Example:

A plumber will fix burst pipes, but they won't repair waterlogged appliances.

Plumbers will fix burst pipes, but they won't repair waterlogged appliances.

1. When a taxpayer is waiting to receive a tax refund from the Internal

   Revenue Service, you begin to notice what time the mail carrier arrives.

2. If the taxpayer does not receive a refund check within six weeks of fil-

   ing a return, they may not have followed the rules of the IRS.

3. If a taxpayer does not include the Social Security number on a return,

   you will have to wait for a refund.

4. When taxpayers do not file their return early, they will not get a

   refund quickly.

5. If one has made errors on the tax form, they might even be audited,

thereby delaying a refund even longer.

MODIFIERS

Exercise 35   REVISING: ADJECTIVES AND ADVERBS
Handbook sections 19a—19b, p. 70

Revise the following sentences to use adjectives and adverbs appropriately. If any sentence is correct as given, circle the number preceding it.

Example:

The announcer warned that traffic was moving very slow.

The announcer warned that traffic was moving very slowly.

1. The eighteenth-century essayist Samuel Johnson fared bad in his early

   life.

2. Johnson's family was poor, his hearing was bad, and he received little

   education.

3. After failing as a schoolmaster, Johnson moved to London, where he

   did good.

4. Johnson was taken serious as a critic and dictionary maker.

5. Johnson was real surprised when he received a pension from King

   George III.

Exercise 36   REVISING: COMPARATIVES AND SUPERLATIVES
Handbook section 19c, p. 71

Revise the following sentences so that the comparative and superlative forms of adjectives and adverbs are appropriate for formal usage.

Example:

Attending classes full-time and working at two jobs was the most impossible thing I ever did.

Attending classes full-time and working at two jobs was impossible [*or the hardest thing I ever did*].

1. The Brontë sisters are considered some of the better writers of their

    period.

2. Some readers think Emily Brontë's *Wuthering Heights* is the most sad-

    dest novel they have ever read.

3. Many critics praise Emily more than the other two sisters, Charlotte

    and Anne.

4. Critics still argue about whether Charlotte or Emily wrote more

    better.

5. Certainly this family of women novelists was the most unique.

Exercise 37   REVISING: PRESENT AND PAST PARTICIPLES (ESL)
Handbook section 19e, p. 72

Revise the adjectives in the following sentences as needed to distinguish between present and past participles. If the sentence is correct as given, circle the number preceding it.

Example:

The subject was embarrassed to many people.

The subject was <u>embarrassing</u> to many people.

1. Several critics found Alice Walker's *The Color Purple* to be a fascinated book.

2. One confused critic wished that Walker had deleted the scenes set in Africa.

3. Another critic argued that although the book contained many depressed episodes, the overall effect was excited.

4. Since other readers found the book annoyed, this critic pointed out its many surprising qualities.

5. In the end most critics agreed that the book was a satisfied novel about the struggles of an African American woman.

Exercise 38   REVISING: ARTICLES (ESL)
Handbook section 19f, p. 72

For each blank, indicate whether *a, an, the,* or no article should be inserted.

Example:

On our bicycle trip across _____ country, we carried _____ map and plenty of _____ food and _____ water.

On our bicycle trip across <u>the</u> country, we carried <u>a</u> map and plenty of food and water.

From _____ native American Indians who migrated from _____ Asia 20,000 years ago to _____ new arrivals who now come by _____ planes, _____ United States is _____ nation of foreigners. It is _____ country of immigrants who are all living under _____ single flag.

Back in _____ seventeenth and eighteenth centuries, at least 75 percent of the population came from _____ England. However, between 1820 and 1975 more than 38 million immigrants came to this country from elsewhere in _____ Europe. Many children of _____ immigrants were self-conscious and denied their heritage; many even refused to learn _____ native language of their parents and grandparents. They tried to "Americanize" themselves. The so-called Melting Pot theory of _____ social change stressed _____ importance of blending everyone together into _____ kind of stew. Each nationality would contribute its own flavor, but _____ final stew would be something called "American."

This Melting Pot theory was never completely successful. In the last half of the twentieth century, _____ ethnic revival changed _____ metaphor. Many people now see _____ American society as _____ mosaic. Americans are once again proud of their heritage, and _____ ethnic differences make _____ mosaic colorful and interesting.

Exercise 39   REVISING: MISPLACED MODIFIERS
Handbook section 20a, p. 74

Revise the following sentences so that modifiers clearly modify the intended words.

Example:

I came to enjoy flying over time.

Over time I came to enjoy flying.

1. Women have contributed much to American culture of great value.

2. For example, Elizabeth Pinckney during the colonial era introduced indigo, the source of a valuable blue dye.

3. Emma Willard founded the Troy Female Seminary, the first institution to provide a college-level education for women in 1821.

4. Mary Lyon founded Mount Holyoke Female Seminary as the first true women's college with directors and a campus who would sustain the college even after Lyon's death.

5. *Una* was the first US newspaper, which was founded by Pauline Wright Davis in 1853, that was dedicated to gaining women's rights.

6. Mitchell's Comet was discovered in 1847, which was named for Maria Mitchell.

7. Mitchell was the first American woman astronomer who lived from 1818 to 1889.

8. She was a member at Vassar College of the first faculty.

9. She was when elected to the American Academy of Arts and Sciences in 1848 the first woman to join the prestigious organization.

10. Mitchell said that she was persistent rather than especially capable when asked about her many accomplishments.

Exercise 40   REVISING: DANGLING MODIFIERS
Handbook section 20b, p. 76

Revise the following sentences to eliminate any dangling modifiers. Each item has more than one possible answer.

Example:

Driving north, the vegetation became more sparse.

Driving north, <u>we noticed</u> that the vegetation became more sparse.

<u>As we drove north,</u> the vegetation became more sparse.

1. After accomplishing many deeds of valor, Andrew Jackson's fame led to his election to the presidency in 1828 and 1832.

2. At the age of fourteen, both of Jackson's parents died.

3. To aid the American Revolution, service as a mounted courier was Jackson's choice.

4. After being struck with a saber by a British officer, Jackson's craggy face bore a scar.

5. Though not well educated, a successful career as a lawyer and judge proved Jackson's ability.

6. Winning many military battles, the American public believed in Jackson's leadership.

7. Earning the nicknames "Old Hickory" and "Sharp Knife," the War of 1812 established Jackson's military prowess.

8. Losing only six dead and ten wounded, the triumph of the Battle of New Orleans burnished Jackson's reputation.

9. After putting down raiding parties from Florida, Jackson's victories helped pressure Spain to cede that territory.

10. While briefly governor of Florida, the US presidency became Jackson's goal.

SENTENCE FAULTS

Exercise 41   IDENTIFYING AND REVISING SENTENCE FRAGMENTS
Handbook Chapter 21, pp. 77–79

Apply the tests for completeness to each of the following word groups. If a word group is a complete sentence, circle the number preceding it. If it is a sentence fragment, revise it in two ways: by making it a complete sentence, and by combining it with a main clause written from the information given in other items.

Example:

And could not find his money.
The word group has a verb (*could . . . find*) but no subject.

Revised into a complete sentence:
And he could not find his money.

Combined with a new main clause:
He was lost and could not find his money.

1. In an interesting article about vandalism against works of art.

2. The motives of the vandals varying widely.

3. Those who harm artwork are usually angry.

4. But not necessarily at the artist or the owner.

5. For instance, a man who hammered at Michelangelo's *Pietà*.

6. And knocked off the Virgin Mary's nose.

7. Because he was angry at the Roman Catholic Church.

8. Which knew nothing of his grievance.

9. Although many damaged works can be repaired.

10. Usually even the most skillful repairs are forever visible.

Exercise 42   REVISING: SENTENCE FRAGMENTS
Handbook Chapter 21, pp. 77–79

Revise the following paragraphs to eliminate sentence fragments by combining them with main clauses or rewriting them as main clauses.

Example:

Competent and motivated managers. They are very important. As a component of any baseball team's success.

Competent and motivated managers are a very important component of any baseball team's success.

People generally avoid eating mushrooms except those they buy in

stores. But in fact many varieties of mushrooms are edible. Mushrooms are

members of a large group of vegetation called nonflowering plants.

Including algae, mosses, ferns, and coniferous trees. Even the giant redwoods of California. Most of the nonflowering plants prefer moist environments. Such as forest floors, fallen timber, and still water. Mushrooms, for example. They prefer moist, shady soil. Algae grow in water.

Most mushrooms, both edible and inedible, are members of a class called basidium fungi. A term referring to their method of reproduction. The basidia produce spores. Which can develop into mushrooms. This classification including the prized meadow mushroom, cultivated commercially, and the amanitas. The amanita group contains both edible and poisonous species. Another familiar group of mushrooms, the puffballs. They are easily identified by their round shape. Their spores are contained under a thick skin. Which eventually ruptures to release the spores. The famous morels are in still another group. These pitted, spongy mushrooms called sac fungi because the spores develop in sacs.

Anyone interested in mushrooms as food should heed the US Public Health Service warning. Not to eat any wild mushrooms unless their identity and edibility are established without a doubt.

Exercise 43   REVISING: COMMA SPLICES AND FUSED SENTENCES
Handbook Chapter 22, pp. 79–81

Correct each comma splice or fused sentence below in two of the following ways: (1) make separate sentences of the main clauses; (2) insert an appropriate coordinating conjunction or both a comma and a coordinating conjunction between the main clauses; (3) insert a semicolon and a conjunctive adverb or transitional expression between the main clauses; or (4) subordinate one clause to another. If an item contains no fused sentence or comma splice, circle the number preceding it.

Example:

Carolyn still had a headache, she could not get the child-proof cap off the aspirin bottle.

Carolyn still had a headache because she could not get the child-proof cap off the aspirin bottle. [Subordination.]

Carolyn still had a headache, for she could not get the child-proof cap off the aspirin bottle. [Coordinating conjunction.]

1. Money has a long history, it goes back at least as far as the earliest records.

2. Many of the earliest records concern financial transactions, indeed, early history must often be inferred from commercial activity.

3. Every known society has had a system of money, though the objects serving as money have varied widely.

4. Sometimes the objects have had real value, in modern times their value has been more abstract.

5. Cattle, fermented beverages, and rare shells have served as money each one had actual value for the society.

6. As money, these objects acquired additional value they represented other goods.

7. Today money may be made of worthless paper, it may even consist of a bit of data in a computer's memory.

8. We think of money as valuable only our common faith in it makes it valuable.

9. That faith is sometimes fragile, consequently, currencies themselves are fragile.

10. Economic crises often shake the belief in money, indeed, such weakened faith helped cause the Great Depression of the 1930s.

11. Throughout history money and religion were closely linked, there was little distinction between government and religion.

12. The head of state and the religious leader were often the same person so that all power rested in one ruler.

13. These powerful leaders decided what objects would serve as money, their backing encouraged public faith in the money.

14. Coins were minted of precious metals the religious overtones of money were then strengthened.

15. People already believed the precious metals to be divine, their use in money intensified its allure.

Exercise 44   REVISING: COMMA SPLICES AND FUSED SENTENCES
Handbook Chapter 22, pp. 79–81

Identify and revise the comma splices and fused sentences in the following paragraph.

Example:

Many people are happy to leave their student days behind them, however, some miss the stimulation of academic courses.

Many people are happy to leave their student days behind them; however, some miss the stimulation of academic courses.

Many people are happy to leave their student days behind them. However, some miss the stimulation of academic courses.

All those parents who urged their children to eat broccoli were right, the vegetable really is healthful. Broccoli contains sulforaphane, moreover, this mustard oil can be found in kale and Brussels sprouts. Sulforaphane causes the body to make an enzyme that attacks carcinogens, these substances cause cancer. The enzyme speeds up the work of the kidneys then they can flush harmful chemicals out of the body. Other vegetables have similar benefits however, green, leafy vegetables like broccoli are the most efficient. Thus, wise people will eat their broccoli it could save their lives.

III
Punctuation

Exercise 45 USING THE COMMA BETWEEN LINKED MAIN CLAUSES
Handbook section 23a, p. 85

Insert a comma before each coordinating conjunction that links main clauses in the following sentences.

> *Example:*
>
> I would have attended the concert and the reception but I had to baby-sit for my niece.
>
> I would have attended the concert and the reception, but I had to baby-sit for my niece.

1. Parents once automatically gave their children the father's last name but some no longer do.

2. Parents may now give their children any last name they choose and the arguments for choosing the mother's last name are often strong and convincing.

3. The child's last name may be just the mother's or it may link the mother's and the father's with a hyphen.

4. Sometimes the first and third children will have the mother's last name and the second child will have the father's.

5. Occasionally, the mother and father combine parts of their names and a new last name is formed.

Exercise 46   USING THE COMMA WITH INTRODUCTORY ELEMENTS
Handbook section 23b, p. 85

Insert commas where needed after introductory elements in the following sentences. If a sentence is punctuated correctly as given, circle the number preceding it.

Example:

After the new library opened the old one became a student union.

After the new library opened, the old one became a student union.

1. Veering sharply to the right a large flock of birds neatly avoids a high wall.

2. Moving in a fluid mass is typical of flocks of birds and schools of fish.

3. With the help of complex computer simulations zoologists are learning more about this movement.

4. As it turns out evading danger is really an individual response.

5. Multiplied over hundreds of individuals these responses look as if they have been choreographed.

Exercise 47   PUNCTUATING ESSENTIAL AND NONESSENTIAL ELEMENTS
Handbook section 23c, p. 86

Insert commas in the following sentences to set off nonessential elements, and delete any commas that incorrectly set off essential elements. If a sentence is correct as given, circle the number preceding it.

Example:

Elizabeth Blackwell who attended medical school in the 1840s was the first American woman to earn a medical degree.

Elizabeth Blackwell, who attended medical school in the 1840s, was the first American woman to earn a medical degree.

1. Italians insist that Marco Polo the thirteenth-century explorer did not import pasta from China.

2. Pasta which consists of flour and water and often egg existed in Italy long before Marco Polo left for his travels.

3. A historian who studied pasta says that it originated in the Middle East in the fifth century.

4. Most Italians dispute this account although their evidence is shaky.

5. Wherever it originated, the Italians are now the undisputed masters, in making and cooking pasta.

6. Marcella Hazan, who has written several books on Italian cooking, insists that homemade and hand-rolled pasta is the best.

7. Most cooks buy dried pasta lacking the time to make their own.

8. The finest pasta is made from semolina, a flour from hard durum wheat.

9. Pasta manufacturers choose hard durum wheat, because it makes firmer cooked pasta than common wheat does.

10. Pasta, made from common wheat, gets soggy in boiling water.

Exercise 48   USING THE COMMA WITH SERIES AND ADJECTIVES
Handbook sections 23d–23e, p. 88

Insert commas in the following sentences to separate coordinate adjectives or elements in series. Circle the number preceding any sentence whose punctuation is correct.

Example:

Although quiet by day, the club became a noisy smoky dive at night.

Although quiet by day, the club became a noisy, smoky dive at night.

1. Shoes with high heels were originally designed to protect feet from mud garbage and animal waste in the streets.

2. The first known high heels worn strictly for fashion appeared in the sixteenth century.

3. The heels were worn by men and made of colorful silk fabrics soft suedes or smooth leathers.

4. High-heeled shoes became popular when the short powerful King Louis XIV of France began wearing them.

5. Louis's influence was so strong that men and women of the court priests and cardinals and even household servants wore high heels.

Exercise 49   USING THE COMMA WITH QUOTATIONS
Handbook section 23g, p. 89

Insert commas or semicolons in the following sentences to correct punctuation with quotations. Circle the number preceding any sentence whose punctuation is correct.

Example:

The shoplifter declared "I didn't steal anything."

The shoplifter declared, "I didn't steal anything."

1. The writer and writing teacher Peter Elbow suggests that an "open-ended writing process . . . can change you, not just your words."

2. "I think of the open-ended writing process as a voyage in two stages" Elbow says.

3. "The sea voyage is a process of divergence, branching, proliferation, and confusion" Elbow continues "the coming to land is a process of convergence, pruning, centralizing, and clarifying."

4. "Keep up one session of writing long enough to get loosened up and tired" advises Elbow "long enough in fact to make a bit of a voyage."

5. "In coming to new land" Elbow says "you develop a new conception of what you are writing about."

Exercise 50   **REVISING: NEEDLESS AND MISUSED COMMAS**
Handbook Chapter 23, pp. 85–89

Revise the following sentences to eliminate needless or misused commas. Circle the number preceding any sentence that is punctuated correctly.

Example:

The large portrait, that hung in the dining hall, was stolen by pranksters.

The large portrait_that hung in the dining hall_was stolen by pranksters.

1. Nearly 32 million US residents, speak a first language other than English.

2. After English the languages most commonly spoken in the United States are, Spanish, French, and German.

3. Almost 75 percent of the people, who speak foreign languages, used the words, "good," or "very good," when judging their proficiency in English.

4. Recent immigrants, especially those speaking Spanish, Chinese, and Korean, tended to judge their English more harshly.

5. The states with the highest proportion of foreign-language speakers, are New Mexico, and California.

Exercise 51   **REVISING: COMMAS**
Handbook Chapter 23, pp. 85–89

Insert commas in the following paragraphs wherever they are needed, and eliminate any misused or needless commas.

Example:

A recent newspaper article pointed out, that many historic buildings, monuments, and landmarks, have become tourist sites.

A recent newspaper article pointed out_that many historic buildings, monuments, and landmarks_have become tourist sites.

Ellis Island New York reopened for business in 1990 but now the customers are tourists not immigrants. This spot which lies in New York Harbor was the first American soil seen, or touched by many of the nation's immigrants. Though other places also served as ports of entry for foreigners none has the symbolic power of, Ellis Island. Between its opening in 1892 and its closing in 1954, over 20 million people about two-thirds of all immigrants were detained there before taking up their new lives in the United States. Ellis Island processed over 2000 newcomers a day when immigration was at its peak between 1900 and 1920.

As the end of a long voyage and the introduction to the New World Ellis Island must have left something to be desired. The "huddled masses" as the Statue of Liberty calls them indeed were huddled. New arrivals were herded about kept standing in lines for hours or days yelled at and abused. Assigned numbers they submitted their bodies to the pokings and proddings of the silent nurses and doctors, who were charged with ferreting out the slightest sign, of sickness disability or insanity. That test having been passed the immigrants faced interrogation by an official through an interpreter. Those, with names deemed inconveniently long or difficult to pronounce, often found themselves permanently labeled with abbreviations, of their names, or with the names, of their hometowns. But, millions survived the examination humiliation and confusion, to take the last short boat ride to New York City. For many of them and especially for their descendants Ellis Island eventually became not a nightmare but the place where a new life began.

Exercise 52   USING THE SEMICOLON BETWEEN MAIN CLAUSES
Handbook sections 24a–24b, p. 90

Insert semicolons in the following sentences to separate main clauses. If the clauses are related by a conjunctive adverb, insert a comma or commas where needed to set off the adverb.

Example:

Music is a form of communication like language the basic elements however are not letters but notes.

Music is a form of communication like language; the basic elements, however, are not letters but notes.

1. Computers can process any information that can be represented numerically consequently they can process musical information.

2. A computer's ability to process music depends on what software it can run furthermore it must be connected to a system that converts electrical vibration into sound.

3. Computers and their sound systems can produce many different sounds in fact the number of possible sounds is infinite.

4. Musicians have always experimented with new technology audiences have always resisted the experiments.

5. The computer is not the first new technology in music indeed the pipe organ and saxophone were also technological breakthroughs in their day.

6. Most computer musicians are not merely following the latest fad they are discovering new sounds and new ways to manipulate sound.

7. More and more musicians are playing computerized instruments more and more listeners are worrying about the future of acoustic instruments.

8. Few musicians have abandoned acoustic instruments most value acoustic sounds as much as electronic sounds.

9. The powerful music computers are very expensive they are therefore used only by professional musicians.

10. These music computers are too expensive for the average consumer however digital keyboards can be less expensive and are widely available.

Exercise 53   **REVISING: SEMICOLONS**
Handbook Chapter 24, pp. 89–91

Insert semicolons in the following paragraph wherever they are needed. Eliminate any misused or needless semicolons, substituting other punctuation as appropriate.

Example:

The final night of the horror film series left the audience; chilled, terrified, and quivering with delight.

The final night of the horror film series left the audience_chilled, terrified, and quivering with delight.

The set, sounds, and actors in the movie captured the essence of horror films. The set was ideal; dark, deserted streets, trees dipping their branches over the sidewalks, mist hugging the ground and creeping up to meet the trees, looming shadows of unlighted, turreted houses. The sounds, too, were appropriate, especially terrifying was the hard, hollow sound of footsteps echoing throughout the film. But the best feature of the movie was its actors; all of them tall, pale, and thin to the point of emaciation. With one exception, they were dressed uniformly in gray and had gray hair. The exception was an actress who dressed only in black; as if to set off her pale yellow, nearly white, long hair; the only color in the film. The glinting black eyes of another actor stole almost every scene, indeed, they were the source of the film's mischief.

Exercise 54   REVISING: COLONS AND SEMICOLONS
Handbook Chapters 24–25, pp. 89–92

In the following sentences, use colons or semicolons where they are need-ed, and delete or replace them where they are incorrect.

Example:

Mix the ingredients as follows sift the flour and salt together, add the milk, and slowly beat in the egg yolk.

Mix the ingredients as follows: sift the flour and salt together, add the milk, and slowly beat in the egg yolk.

1. Sunlight is made up of three kinds of radiation; visible rays; infrared rays, which we cannot see; and ultraviolet rays, which are also invisible.

2. Especially in the ultraviolet range; sunlight is harmful to the eyes.

3. Ultraviolet rays can damage the retina: furthermore, they can cause cataracts on the lens.

4. Infrared rays are the longest; measuring 700 nonometers and longer, while ultraviolet rays are the shortest; measuring 400 nanometers and shorter.

5. The lens protects the eye by: absorbing much of the ultraviolet radi-ation and thus shielding the retina.

6. By protecting the retina, however, the lens becomes a victim; growing cloudy and blocking vision.

7. The best way to protect your eyes is: to wear hats that shade the face and sunglasses that screen out the ultraviolet rays.

8. Many sunglass lenses have been designed as ultraviolet screens; many others are extremely ineffective.

9. Sunglass lenses should screen out ultraviolet rays and be dark enough so that people can't see your eyes through them, otherwise, the lenses will not protect your eyes, and you will be at risk for cataracts later in life.

10. People who spend much time outside in the sun; really owe it to themselves to buy a pair of sunglasses that will shield their eyes.

Exercise 55   **REVISING: APOSTROPHES**
Handbook Chapter 26, pp. 92–94

In the following paragraph, correct any mistakes in the use of apostrophes and any confusion between contractions and possessive personal pronouns.

Example:

Many developing nations' are struggling to improve they're citizens standard's of living.

Many developing nations are struggling to improve their citizens' standards of living.

People who's online eperiences include blogging, Web cams, and social-networking sites are often used to seeing the details of other peoples private lives. Many are also comfortable sharing they're own opinions, photographs, and videos with family, friend's and even stranger's. However, they need to realize that employers and even the government can see they're information, too. Employers commonly put applicants names through social-networking Web sites such as *MySpace* and *Facebook*. Many companies monitor their employees outbound e-mail. People can take steps to protect their personal information by adjusting the privacy settings on their

social-networking pages. They can avoid posting photos of themselves that

they wouldnt want an employer to see. They can avoid sending personal e-

mail while their at work. Its the individuals responsibility to keep certain

information private.

Exercise 56   REVISING: QUOTATION MARKS
Handbook Chapter 27, pp. 94–97

Insert quotation marks as needed in the following paragraph.

Example:

One course, titled Literature, Politics, and Society, includes everything
from Plato's *Republic* to Bush's declaration of war on terrorism.

One course, titled "Literature, Politics, and Society," includes everything
from Plato's *Republic* to Bush's declaration of war on terrorism.

In one class we talked about a passage from I Have a Dream, the

speech delivered by Martin Luther King, Jr., on the steps of the Lincoln

Memorial on August 28, 1963:

> When the architects of our republic wrote the magnificent
>
> words of the Constitution and the Declaration of Independence,
>
> they were signing a promissory note to which every American
>
> was to fall heir. This note was a promise that all men would be
>
> guaranteed the unalienable rights of life, liberty, and the pursuit
>
> of happiness.

What did Dr. King mean by this statement? the teacher asked. Per-

haps we should define promissory note first. Then she explained that a person who signs such a note agrees to pay a specific sum of money on a particular date or on demand by the holder of the note.

One student suggested, Maybe Dr. King meant that the writers of the Constitution and Declaration promised that all people in America should be equal.

He and over 200,000 people had gathered in Washington, DC, added another student. Maybe their purpose was to demand payment, to demand those rights for African Americans.

The whole discussion was an eye-opener for those of us (including me) who had never considered that those documents make promises that we should expect our country to fulfill.

Exercise 57   REVISING: END PUNCTUATION
Handbook Chapter 28, pp. 97–98

Insert appropriate end punctuation (periods, question marks, or exclamation points) where needed in the following paragraph.

Example:

Noticing my luggage, the bus driver asked where I was from?

Noticing my luggage, the bus driver asked where I was from.

When visitors first arrive in Hawaii, they often encounter an unexpected language barrier Standard English is the language of business and government, but many of the people speak Pidgin English Instead of an excited "Aloha" the visitors may be greeted with an excited Pidgin "Howzit" or asked if they know "how fo' find one good hotel" Many Hawaiians question whether Pidgin will hold children back because it prevents communication with *haoles*, or Caucasians, who run businesses Yet many others feel

that Pidgin is a last defense of ethnic diversity on the islands To those who

want to make standard English the official language of the state, these

Hawaiians may respond, "Just 'cause I speak Pidgin no mean I dumb"

They may ask, "Why you no listen" or, in standard English, "Why don't

you listen"

Exercise 58   USING ELLIPSIS MARKS
Handbook section 29c, p. 99

Use ellipsis marks and any other needed punctuation to follow the numbered instructions for quoting from the following paragraph.

> Women in the sixteenth and seventeenth centuries were educat-
> ed in the home and, in some cases, in boarding schools. Men were
> educated at home, in grammar schools, and at the universities. The
> universities were closed to female students. For women, "learning the
> Bible," as Elizabeth Joceline puts it, was an impetus to learning to
> read. To be able to read the Bible in the vernacular was a liberating
> experience that freed the reader from hearing only the set passages
> read in the church and interpreted by the church. A Protestant
> woman was expected to read the scriptures daily, to meditate on
> them, and to memorize portions of them. In addition, a woman was
> expected to instruct her entire household in "learning the Bible" by
> holding instructional and devotional times each day for all household
> members, including the servants.
>
> —Charlotte F. Otten, *English Women's Voices, 1540–1700*

1. Quote the fifth sentence, but omit everything from *that freed the read-*

er to the end.

2. Quote the fifth sentence, but omit the words *was a liberating experience that.*

3. Quote the first and sixth sentences.

Exercise 59   REVISING: PUNCTUATION
Handbook Chapters 23–29, pp. 85–102

The following paragraphs are unpunctuated except for end-of-sentence periods. Insert commas, semicolons, apostrophes, quotation marks, colons, dashes, or parentheses where they are required. When different marks would be appropriate in the same place, be able to defend the choice you make.

Example:

As an advertisement once put it The best way to start a day is with a good cup of coffee.

As an advertisement once put it, "The best way to start a day is with a good cup of coffee."

Brewed coffee is the most widely consumed beverage in the world. The trade in coffee beans alone amounts to well over $6000000000 a year and the total volume of beans traded exceeds 4250000 tons a year. Its believed that the beverage was introduced into Arabia in the fifteenth century AD probably by Ethiopians. By the middle or late sixteenth century the Arabs had introduced the beverage to the Europeans who at first resisted it because of its strong flavor and effect as a mild stimulant. The French Italians and other Europeans incorporated coffee into their diets by the seventeenth century the English however preferred tea which they were then importing from India. Since America was colonized primarily by the English Americans also preferred tea. Only after the Boston Tea Party 1773 did Americans begin drinking coffee in large quantities. Now though the US is one of the top coffee-consuming countries consumption having been spurred on by familiar advertising claims Good till the last drop Rich hearty aroma Always rich never bitter.

Produced from the fruit of an evergreen tree coffee is grown primarily in Latin America southern Asia and Africa. Coffee trees require a hot climate high humidity rich soil with good drainage and partial shade consequently they thrive on the east or west slopes of tropical volcanic mountains where the soil is laced with potash and drains easily. The coffee beans actually seeds grow inside bright red berries. The berries are picked by hand and the beans are extracted by machine leaving a pulpy fruit residue that can be used for fertilizer. The beans are usually roasted in ovens a chemical process that releases the beans essential oil caffeol which gives coffee its distinctive aroma. Over a hundred different varieties of beans are produced in the world each with a different flavor attributable to three factors the species of plant *Coffea arabia* and *Coffea robusta* are the most common and the soil and climate where the variety was grown.

IV
Spelling and Mechanics

Exercise 60   SMALL CAPS USING CORRECT SPELLINGS
Handbook section 30b, p. 105

Select the correct spelling from the choices in brackets.

Example:

The boat [passed, past] us so fast that we rocked violently in [its, it's] wake.

The boat passed us so fast that we rocked violently in its wake.

1. Science [affects, effects] many [important, importent] aspects of our lives.

2. Many people have a [pore, poor] understanding of the [role, roll] of scientific breakthroughs in [their, they're] health.

3. Many people [beleive, believe] that [docters, doctors] are more [responsable, responsible] for [improvements, improvments] in health care than scientists are.

4. But scientists in the [labratory, laboratory] have made crucial steps in the search for [knowlege, knowledge] about health and [medecine, medicine].

5. For example, one scientist [who's, whose] discoveries have [affected, effected] many people is Ulf Von Euler.

6. In the 1950s Von Euler's discovery of certain hormones [lead, led] to the invention of the birth control pill.

7. Von Euler's work was used by John Rock, who [developed, developped] the first birth control pill and influenced family [planing, planning].

8. Von Euler also discovered the [principal, principle] neurotransmitter that controls the heartbeat.

9. Another scientist, Hans Selye, showed what [affect, effect] stress can have on the body.

10. His findings have [lead, led] to methods of [baring, bearing] stress.

Exercise 61   **REVISING: HYPHENS**
Handbook section 30c, p. 107

Insert hyphens wherever they are needed, and delete them where they are not needed. If a sentence is correct as given, circle the number preceding it.

Example:

Elephants have twelve inch long teeth, but they have only four of them.

Elephants have twelve-inch-long teeth, but they have only four of them.

1. The African elephant is well known for its size.

2. Both male and female African elephants can grow to a ten-foot height.

3. The non African elephants of south central Asia are somewhat smaller.

4. A fourteen or fifteen year old elephant has reached sexual maturity.

5. The elephant life span is about sixty five or seventy years.

6. A newborn elephant calf weighs two to three hundred pounds.

7. It stands about thirty three inches high.

8. A two hundred pound, thirty three inch baby is quite a big baby.

9. Unfortunately, elephants are often killed for their ivory tusks, and partly as a result they are an increasingly-endangered species.

10. African governments have made tusk and ivory selling illegal.

Exercise 62   **REVISING: CAPITAL LETTERS**
Handbook Chapter 31, pp. 108–10

Edit the following sentences to correct errors in capitalization. Consult a dictionary if you are in doubt. If a sentence is correct as given, circle the number preceding it.

Example:

The first book on the reading list is mark twain's *a connecticut yankee in king arthur's court.*

The first book on the reading list is Mark Twain's *A Connecticut Yankee in King Arthur's Court.*

1. San Antonio, texas, is a thriving city in the southwest.

2. The city has always offered much to tourists interested in the roots of spanish settlement of the new world.

3. The alamo is one of five Catholic Missions built by Priests to convert native americans and to maintain spain's claims in the area.

4. But the alamo is more famous for being the site of an 1836 battle that helped to create the republic of Texas.

5. Many of the nearby Streets, such as Crockett street, are named for men who died in that Battle.

6. The Hemisfair plaza and the San Antonio river link tourist and convention facilities.

7. Restaurants, Hotels, and shops line the River. the haunting melodies of "Una paloma blanca" and "malagueña" lure passing tourists into Casa rio and other mexican restaurants.

8. The university of Texas at San Antonio has expanded, and a Medical Center lies in the Northwest part of the city.

9. Sea World, on the west side of San Antonio, entertains grandparents, fathers and mothers, and children with the antics of dolphins and seals.

10. The City has attracted high-tech industry, creating a corridor between san antonio and austin.

Exercise 63   **Revising: Italics or underlining**
Handbook Chapter 32, pp. 110–12

In the following sentences, circle (1) the words and phrases that need highlighting with italics or underlining and (2) the words and phrases that are highlighted unnecessarily. If a sentence is correct as given, circle the number preceding it.

Example:

Of Hitchcock's movies, Psycho is the scariest.

Of Hitchcock's movies, (Psycho) is the scariest.

1. Of the many Vietnam veterans who are writers, Oliver Stone is perhaps the most famous for writing and directing the films Platoon and Born on the Fourth of July.

2. Tim O'Brien has written short stories for Esquire, GQ, and Massachusetts Review.

3. Going After Cacciato is O'Brien's dreamlike novel about the horrors of combat.

4. The word Vietnam is technically two words (*Viet* and *Nam*), but most American writers spell it as *one* word.

5. American writers use words or phrases borrowed from Vietnamese, such as di di mau ("go quickly") or dinky dau ("crazy").

6. Philip Caputo's *gripping* account of his service in Vietnam appears in the book A Rumor of War.

7. Caputo's book was made into a television movie, also titled *A Rumor of War.*

8. David Rabe's plays—including The Basic Training of Pavlo Hummel, Streamers, and Sticks and Bones—depict the effects of the war *not only* on the soldiers *but also* on their families.

9. Called the *poet laureate of the Vietnam war*, Steve Mason has published two collections of poems: Johnny's Song and Warrior for Peace.

10. The Washington Post published *rave* reviews of Veteran's Day, an autobiography by Rod Kane.

Exercise 64   REVISING: ABBREVIATIONS
   Handbook Chapter 33, pp. 112–13

Revise the following sentences as needed to correct inappropriate use of abbreviations for nontechnical writing. If a sentence is correct as given, circle the number preceding it.

Example:

One prof. lectured for five hrs.

One professor lectured for five hours.

1. In an issue of *Science* magazine, Dr. Virgil L. Sharpton discusses a theory that could help explain the extinction of dinosaurs.

2. About 65 mill. yrs. ago, a comet or asteroid crashed into the earth.

3. The result was a huge crater about 10 km. (6.2 mi.) deep in the Gulf of Mex.

4. Sharpton's new measurements suggest that the crater is 50 pct. larger than scientists had previously believed.

5. Indeed, 20-yr.-old drilling cores reveal that the crater is about 186 mi. wide, roughly the size of Conn.

6. The space object was traveling more than 100,000 miles per hour and hit the earth with the impact of 100 to 300 million megatons of TNT.

7. On impact, 200,000 cubic km. of rock and soil were vaporized or thrown into the air.

8. That's the equivalent of 2.34 bill. cubic ft. of matter.

9. The impact would have created 400-ft. tidal waves across the Atl. Ocean, temps. higher than 20,000 degs., and powerful earthquakes.

10. Sharpton theorizes that the dust, vapor, and smoke from this impact blocked the sun's rays for mos., cooled the earth, and thus resulted in the death of the dinosaurs.

Exercise 65   **REVISING: NUMBERS**
Handbook Chapter 34, pp. 113–14

Revise the following sentences so that numbers are used appropriately for nontechnical writing. If a sentence is correct as given, circle the number preceding it.

Example:

Addie paid two hundred and five dollars for used scuba gear.

Addie paid $205 for used scuba gear.

1. The planet Saturn is nine hundred million miles, or nearly one billion five hundred million kilometers, from the sun.

2. A year on Saturn equals almost thirty of our years.

3. Thus, Saturn orbits the sun only two and four-tenths times during the average human life span.

4. It travels in its orbit at about twenty-one thousand six hundred miles per hour.

5. 15 to 20 times denser than Earth's core, Saturn's core measures 17,000 miles across.

6. The temperature at Saturn's cloud tops is minus one hundred seventy degrees Fahrenheit.

7. In nineteen hundred thirty-three, astronomers found on Saturn's surface a huge white spot 2 times the size of Earth and 7 times the size of Mercury.

8. Saturn's famous rings reflect almost seventy percent of the sunlight that approaches the planet.

9. The ring system is almost forty thousand miles wide, beginning 8,800 miles from the planet's visible surface and ending forty-seven thousand miles from that surface.

10. The spacecraft *Cassini* traveled more than eight hundred and twenty million miles to explore and photograph Saturn.

Exercise 66   SYNTHESIZING SOURCES
Handbook section 37b, p. 141

The three passages below address the same issue, the legalization of drugs. What similarities do you see in the authors' ideas? What differences? Write a paragraph of your own in which you use these authors' views as a point of departure for your own view about drug legalization.

Perhaps the most unfortunate victims of drug prohibition laws have been the residents of America's ghettos. These laws have proved largely futile in deterring ghetto-dwellers from becoming drug abusers, but they do account for much of what ghetto residents identify as the drug problem. Aggressive, gun-toting drug dealers often upset law-abiding residents far more than do addicts nodding out in doorways. Meanwhile other residents perceive the drug dealers as heroes and successful role models. They're symbols of success to children who see no other options. At the same time the increasingly harsh criminal penalties imposed on adult drug dealers have led drug traffickers to recruit juveniles. Where once children started dealing drugs only after they had been using them for a few years, today the sequence is often reversed. Many children start using drugs only after working for older drug dealers for a while. Legalization of drugs, like legalization of alcohol in the early 1930s, would drive the drug-dealing business off the streets and out of apartment buildings and into government-regulated, tax-paying stores. It also would force many of the gun-toting dealers out of the business and convert others into legitimate businessmen.

—Ethan A. Nadelmann, "Shooting Up"

Statistics argue against legalization. The University of Michigan conducts an annual survey of twelfth graders, asking the students about their drug consumption. In 1980, 56.4 percent of those polled said they had used marijuana in the past twelve months, whereas in 2008 only 42 percent had done so. Cocaine use was also reduced in the same period (22.6 percent to 6 percent). At the same time, twelve-month use of legally available drugs—alcohol and nicotine-containing cigarettes—

remained constant at about 75 percent and 55 percent, respectively. The numbers of illegal drug users haven't declined nearly enough: those teenaged marijuana and cocaine users are still vulnerable to addiction and even death, and they threaten to infect their impressionable peers. But clearly the prohibition of illegal drugs has helped, while the legal status of alcohol and cigarettes has not made them less popular.

—Sylvia Runkle, "The Case Against Legalization"

I have to laugh at the debate over what to do about the drug problem. Everyone is running around offering solutions—from making drug use a more serious criminal offense to legalizing it. But there isn't a real solution. I know that. I used and abused drugs, and people, and society, for two decades. Nothing worked to get me to stop all that behavior except just plain being sick and tired. Nothing. Not threats, not ten-plus years in prison, not anything that was said to me. I used until I got through. Period. And that's when you'll win the war. When all the dope fiends are done. Not a minute before.

—Michael W. Posey, "I Did Drugs Until They Wore Me Out. Then I Stopped."

Exercise 67   SUMMARIZING AND PARAPHRASING
Handbook section 38a, p. 142

Prepare two source notes, one summarizing the entire paragraph below and the other paraphrasing the first four sentences (ending with the word *autonomy*).

Federal organization [of the United States] has made it possible for the different states to deal with the same problems in many different ways. One consequence of federalism, then, has been that people are treated differently, by law, from state to state. The great strength of this system is that differences from state to state in cultural preferences, moral standards, and levels of wealth can be accommodated. In contrast to a unitary system in which the central government makes all important decisions (as in France), federalism is a powerful arrangement for maximizing regional freedom and autonomy. The great weakness of our federal system, however, is that people in some states receive less than the best or the most advanced or the least expensive services and policies that government can offer. The federal dilemma does not invite easy solutions, for the costs and benefits of the arrangement have tended to balance out.

—Peter K. Eisinger et al., *American Politics*, p. 44

Exercise 68   COMBINING SUMMARY, PARAPHRASE, AND DIRECT QUOTATION
Handbook section 38a, p. 142

Prepare a source note containing a combination of paraphrase or summary and direct quotation that states the major idea of the passage below.

Most speakers unconsciously duel even during seemingly casual conversations, as can often be observed at social gatherings where they show less concern for exchanging information with other guests than for asserting their own dominance. Their verbal dueling often employs very subtle weapons like mumbling, a hostile act which defeats the listener's desire to understand what the speaker claims he is trying to say (but is really not saying because he is mumbling!). Or the verbal dueler may keep talking after someone has passed out of hearing range—which is often an aggressive challenge to the listener to return and acknowledge the dominance of the speaker.

—Peter K. Farb, *Word Play*, p. 107

Exercise 69   INTEGRATING SOURCES
Handbook Chapter 38, pp. 142–49

Drawing on the ideas in the following paragraph and using examples from your own observations and experiences, write a paragraph about anxiety. Integrate at least one direct quotation and one paraphrase from the following paragraph into your own sentences. In your paragraph identify the author by name and give his credentials: he is a professor of psychiatry and a practicing psychoanalyst.

There are so many ways in which human beings are different from all the lower forms of animals, and almost all of them make us uniquely susceptible to feelings of anxiousness. Our imagination and reasoning powers facilitate anxiety; the anxious feeling is precipitated not by an absolute impending threat—such as the worry about an examination, a speech, travel—but rather by the symbolic and often unconscious representations. We do not have to be experiencing a potential danger. We can experience something related to it. We can recall, through our incredible memories, the original symbolic sense of vulnerability in childhood and suffer the feeling attached to that. We can even forget the original memory and be stuck with the emotion—which is then compounded by its seemingly irrational quality at this time. It is not just the fear of death which pains us, but the anticipation of it; or the anniversary of a specific death; or a street, a hospital, a time of day, a color, a flower, a symbol associated with death.

—Willard Gaylin, "Feeling Anxious," p. 23

Exercise 70 RECOGNIZING PLAGIARISM
Handbook Chapter 39, pp. 150–56

The numbered items below show various attempts to quote or paraphrase the following passage. Carefully compare each attempt with the original passage. Which attempts are plagiarized, inaccurate, or both, and which are acceptable? Why?

> I would agree with the sociologists that psychiatric labeling is dangerous. Society can inflict terrible wounds by discrimination, and by confusing health with disease and disease with badness.
>
> —George E. Vaillant, *Adaptation to Life*, p. 361

1. According to George Vaillant, society often inflicts wounds by using psychiatric labeling, confusing health, disease, and badness (361).

2. According to George Vaillant, "psychiatric labeling [such as 'homosexual' or 'schizophrenic'] is dangerous. Society can inflict terrible wounds by . . . confusing health with disease and disease with badness" (361).

3. According to George Vaillant, when psychiatric labeling discriminates between health and disease or between disease and badness, it can inflict wounds on those labeled (361).

4. Psychiatric labels can badly hurt those labeled, says George Vaillant, because they fail to distinguish among health, illness, and immorality (361).

5. Labels such as "homosexual" and "schizophrenic" can be hurtful when they fail to distinguish among health, illness, and immorality.

6. "I would agree with the sociologists that society can inflict terrible wounds by discrimination, and by confusing health with disease and disease with badness" (Vaillant 361).

Exercise 71   WRITING WORKS-CITED ENTRIES
Handbook section 40b, pp. 162–96

Prepare works-cited entries from the following information. Follow the models of the *MLA Handbook* given in this chapter unless your instructor specifies a different style. For titles, use italics (as here) unless your instructor requests underlining. Arrange the finished entries in alphabetical order. (Do not number entries in a list of works cited.)

1. An article titled "Use of Third Parties to Collect State and Local Taxes on Internet Sales," appearing in the print periodical *The Pacific Business Journal,* volume 5, issue 2, in 2004. The authors are Malai Zimmerman and Kent Hoover. The article appears on pages 45 through 48 of the journal.

2. A government publication you consulted on April 12, 2010, on the Web. The author is the Advisory Commission on Electronic Commerce. The commission is an agency of the United States government. The title of the publication is *Report to Congress.* It was published in April 2005.

3. A Web article with no listed author. The title and sponsor of the Web site is Center on Budget and Policy Priorities. The title of the article is "The Internet Tax Freedom Act and the Digital Divide," and the site is dated September 26, 2007. You consulted the site on April 2, 2010.

4. An article in the magazine *Forbes,* published November 28, 2007, on pages 56 through 58. The author is Janet Novack. The title is "Point, Click, Pay Tax." You accessed the source through the *ProQuest* database on April 10, 2010.

5. A print book titled *All's Fair in Internet Commerce, or Is It?* by Sally G. Osborne. The book was published in 2004 by Random House in New York.

6. An e-mail interview you conducted with Nora James on April 1, 2010.

7. An article titled "State and Local Sales/Use Tax Simplification," appearing on pages 67 through 80 of a print anthology. *The Sales Tax in the Twenty-first Century.* The anthology, is edited by Matthew N. Murray and William F. Fox. The article is by Wayne G. Eggert. The anthology was published in 2004 by Praeger in Westport, Connecticut.

Answers

I. EFFECTIVE SENTENCES

Exercise 1. Revising: Emphasis of subjects and verbs, p. 1

Possible answers

1. <u>Many heroes helped</u> to emancipate the slaves.

2. <u>Harriet Tubman</u>, an escaped slave herself, <u>guided</u> hundreds of other slaves to freedom on the Underground Railroad.

3. <u>Tubman risked</u> a return to slavery or possibly death.

4. During the Civil War <u>she also carried</u> information from the South to the North.

5. After the war, <u>Tubman raised</u> money to help needy former slaves.

Exercise 2. Sentence combining: Emphasis with beginnings and endings, p. 2

Possible answers

1. <u>Pat Taylor strode into the packed room</u>, greeting students called "Taylor's Kids" and nodding to their parents and teachers.

2. <u>This wealthy Louisiana oilman had promised his "Kids" free college educations</u> because he was determined to make higher education available to all qualified but disadvantaged students.

3. <u>The students welcomed Taylor</u>, their voices singing "You Are the Wind Beneath My Wings," their faces flashing with self-confidence.

4. <u>They had thought a college education was beyond their dreams</u>, seeming too costly and too demanding.

5. To help ease the costs and demands of getting to college, <u>Taylor created a bold plan of scholarships, tutoring, and counseling</u>.

Exercise 3. Sentence combining: Coordination, p. 3

Possible revision

1. Many chronic misspellers do not have the time or motivation to master spelling rules. They rely on dictionaries to catch misspellings, but
   most dictionaries list words under their correct spellings. One kind of
   dictionary is designed for chronic misspellers. It lists each word under
   its common *mis*spellings and then provides the correct spelling and
   definition.

2. Henry Hudson was an English explorer, but he captained ships for
   the Dutch East India Company. On a voyage in 1610 he passed
   Greenland and sailed into a great bay in today's northern Canada. He
   thought he and his sailors could winter there, but the cold was terrible
   and food ran out. The sailors mutinied and cast Hudson and eight
   others adrift in a small boat. Hudson and his companions perished.

Exercise 4. Sentence combining: Subordination, p. 4

Possible answers

1. When the bombardier beetle sees an enemy, it shoots out a jet of
   chemicals to protect itself.
   Seeing an enemy, the bombardier beetle shoots out a jet of chemicals
   to protect itself.

2. Consisting of hot and irritating chemicals, the beetle's spray is very
   potent.
   The beetle's spray of hot and irritating chemicals is very potent.

3. Although it is harmless to the beetle, the spray is a most dangerous
   weapon against enemies.
   A most dangerous weapon against enemies, the spray is harmless to
   the beetle.

4. The beetle's spray is a series of tiny chemical explosions discharged as
   a pulsed jet.
   A series of tiny chemical explosions, the beetle's spray is discharged as
   a pulsed jet.

5. Scientists who filmed the beetle discovered that this jet pulses five
   hundred times each second.

Filming the beetle, scientists discovered that this jet pulses some five hundred times each second.

6. Stored separately in the beetle's body and mixed in the spraying gland, the jet's two chemicals resemble a nerve-gas weapon.
    The jet's two chemicals, which are stored separately in the beetle's body and mixed in the spraying gland, resemble a nerve-gas weapon.

7. Revolving like a turret on a World War II bomber, the tip of the beetle's abdomen sprays the chemicals.
    Spraying the chemicals, the tip of the beetle's abdomen revolves like a turret on a World War II bomber.

8. Accompanied by a popping sound, the spray travels twenty-six miles per hour.
    The spray, which is accompanied by a popping sound, travels twenty-six miles per hour.

9. Because the beetle is less than an inch long, it has many enemies.
    Less than an inch long, the beetle has many enemies.

10. Although the beetle defeats most of its enemies, it is still eaten by spiders and birds.
    The beetle defeats most of its enemies except spiders and birds.

Exercise 5. Revising: Coordination and subordination, p. 6

Possible revision

Sir Walter Raleigh personified the Elizabethan Age, the period of Elizabeth I's rule of England, in the last half of the sixteenth century. Raleigh was a courtier, a poet, an explorer, and an entrepreneur. Supposedly, he gained Queen Elizabeth's favor by throwing his cloak beneath her feet at the right moment, just as she was about to step over a puddle. Although there is no evidence for this story, it illustrates Raleigh's dramatic and dynamic personality. His energy drew others to him, and he was one of Elizabeth's favorites. She supported him and dispensed favors to him. However, he lost his queen's goodwill when without her permission he seduced and eventually married one of her maids of honor. After Elizabeth died, her successor, James I, imprisoned Raleigh in the Tower of London on false charges of treason. Raleigh was released after thirteen years but arrested again two years later on the old treason charges. At the age of sixty-six he was beheaded.

Exercise 6. Revising: Empty words and phrases, p. 7

Possible answers

1. *Gerrymandering* involves redrawing the lines of a voting district to benefit a particular party or ethnic group.

2. The name refers to Elbridge Gerry, who as governor of Massachusetts in 1812 redrew voting districts in Essex County.

3. On the map one new district looked like a salamander.

4. Upon seeing the map, a critic of Governor Gerry's administration cried out, "Gerrymander!"

5. Today, a dominant political group may try to change a district's voting pattern by gerrymandering to exclude rival groups' supporters.

Exercise 7. Revising: Unnecessary repetition, p. 8

Possible answers

1. After their tours of duty some Vietnam veterans had problems readjusting to life in America.

2. Afflicted with post-traumatic stress disorder, some veterans had trouble holding jobs and maintaining relationships.

3. Some who used drugs in Vietnam could not break their habits after they returned to the United States.

4. The few veterans who committed crimes and violent acts gained so much notoriety that many Americans thought all veterans were crazy.

5. As a result of such stereotyping, Vietnam-era veterans are protected by antidiscrimination laws.

Exercise 8. Revising: Conciseness, p. 9

Possible answers

1. The Mexican general Antonio López de Santa Anna introduced chewing gum to the United States.

2. After defeat by the Texans in 1854, the exiled general chose to settle in New York.

3. In his baggage the general had stashed a piece of chicle, the dried milky sap of the Mexican sapodilla tree.

4. Santa Anna's friend Thomas Adams brought more of this resin into the country, planning to make rubber.

5. When the plan failed, Adams got a much more successful idea from the way General Santa Anna used the resin, as a gum for chewing.

Exercise 9. Revising: Conciseness, p. 10

Possible answers

After much thought, he concluded that carcinogens could be treated like automobiles. Instead of giving in to a fear of cancer, we should balance the benefits we receive from potential carcinogens (such as plastic and pesticides) against the damage they do. Similarly, instead of responding irrationally to the pollution caused by automobiles, we have decided to live with them and enjoy their benefits while simultaneously working to improve them.

Exercise 10. Revising: Parallelism, p. 11

Possible answers

1. The ancient Greeks celebrated four athletic contests: the Olympic Games at Olympia, the Isthmian Games near Corinth, the Pythian Games at Delphi, and the Nemean Games at Cleonae.

2. Each day the games consisted of either athletic events or ceremonies and sacrifices to the gods.

3. In the years between the games, competitors were taught wrestling, javelin throwing, and boxing.

4. Competitors ran sprints, participated in spectacular chariot and horse races, and ran long distances while wearing full armor.

5. The purpose of such events was to develop physical strength, to demonstrate skill and endurance, and to sharpen the skills needed for war.

6. Events were held <u>both for</u> men and for boys.

7. At the Olympic Games the spectators cheered their favorites to victory, attended sacrifices to the gods, <u>and feasted</u> on the meat not burned
in offerings.

8. The athletes competed less to achieve great wealth than <u>to gain</u> honor
<u>for both</u> themselves and their cities.

9. Of course, exceptional athletes received financial support from patrons,
poems and statues by admiring artists, and <u>even lavish</u> living quarters
from their sponsoring cities.

10. With the medal counts and flag ceremonies, today's Olympians sometimes seem to be proving their countries' superiority more than
<u>demonstrating</u> individual talent.

Exercise 11. Sentence combining: Parallelism, p. 13

Possible answers

1. People can develop post-traumatic stress disorder (PTSD) after experiencing a dangerous situation and fearing for their survival.

2. The disorder can be triggered by a wide variety of events, such as
combat, a natural disaster, or a hostage situation.

3. PTSD can occur immediately after the stressful incident or not until
many years later.

4. Sometimes people with PTSD will act irrationally and angrily.

5. Other symptoms include dreaming that one is reliving the experience,
hallucinating that one is back in the terrifying place, and imagining
that strangers are actually one's former torturers.

6. Victims of the disorder might isolate themselves from family and friends,
stop going to work, commit criminal acts, or do violence to themselves
or others.

7. Victims might need private counseling or hospitalization.

8. The healing process is terrifying when the patients begin but becomes
exciting when they improve.

9. After treatment many patients overcome their fears and seldom experience any recurrence of the symptoms.

10. When victims learn the roots of their fears, they are relieved of their pain, restored to their families, and returned to a productive place in society.

Exercise 12. Revising: Variety, p. 15

Possible revision

After being dormant for many years, the Italian volcano Vesuvius exploded on August 24 in the year AD 79. The ash, pumice, and mud from the volcano buried two towns—Herculaneum and the more famous Pompeii—which lay undiscovered until 1709 and 1748, respectively. The excavation of Pompeii was the more systematic, the occasion for initiating modern methods of conservation and restoration. Whereas Herculaneum was simply looted of its more valuable finds and then left to disintegrate, Pompeii appears much as it did during the eruption. A luxurious house opens onto a lush central garden. An election poster decorates a wall. And a dining table is set for breakfast.

Exercise 13. Revising: Appropriate words, p. 16

Possible answers

1. Acquired immune deficiency syndrome (AIDS) is a serious threat all over the world.

2. The disease is transmitted primarily by sexual intercourse, exchange of bodily fluids, shared needles, and blood transfusions.

3. Those who think the disease is limited to homosexuals, drug users, and foreigners are quite mistaken.

4. Statistics suggest that in the United States one in every five hundred college students carries the HIV virus that causes AIDS.

5. People with HIV or full-blown AIDS do not deserve others' exclusion or callousness. Instead, they need all the compassion, medical care, and financial assistance due the seriously ill.

6. A person with HIV or AIDS often sees a team of doctors or a single doctor with a specialized practice.

7. The doctor may <u>help patients</u> by obtaining social services for them as well as by providing medical care.

8. The <u>person with HIV or AIDS</u> who loses <u>his or her</u> job may need public assistance.

9. For someone who is very ill, a home-care nurse may be necessary. <u>The nurse</u> can administer medications and make the sick person as comfortable as possible.

10. Some people with HIV or AIDS have insurance, but others lack the <u>money</u> for premiums.

Exercise 14. Revising: Exact words, p. 17

1. Maxine Hong Kingston was <u>awarded</u> many prizes for her first two books, *The Woman Warrior* and *China Men.*

2. Kingston <u>cites</u> her mother's tales about ancestors and ancient Chinese customs as the sources of these memoirs.

3. Two of Kingston's <u>progenitors</u> [*or* <u>ancestors</u>], her great-grandfathers, are focal points of *China Men.*

4. Both men led rebellions against <u>oppressive</u> employers: a sugarcane farmer and a railroad-construction supervisor.

5. In her childhood Kingston was greatly <u>affected</u> by her mother's tale about a pregnant aunt who was ostracized by villagers. [*Ostracized* is correct.]

6. The aunt gained <u>vengeance</u> by drowning herself in the village's water supply.

7. Kingston decided to make her nameless relative <u>famous</u> by giving her immortality in *The Woman Warrior.* [*Immortality* is correct.]

8. *Premier* is correct.

9. Both *embody* and *principles* are correct.

10. Kingston's innovative books <u>imply</u> her opposition to racism and sexism both in the China of the past and in the United States of the present.

Exercise 15. Revising: Concrete and specific words, p. 19

Possible revision

I remember as if it were last week how frightened I felt the first time I neared Mrs. Murphy's second-grade class. Just three days before, I had moved from a rural one-street town in Missouri to a suburb of Chicago where the houses and the people were jammed together. My new school looked monstrous from the outside and seemed forbiddingly dim inside as I walked haltingly down the endless corridor toward the classroom. The class was clamorous as I neared the door; but when I slipped inside, twenty faces became still and gawked at me. I felt terrified and longed for a place to hide. However, in a booming voice Mrs. Murphy ordered me to the front of the room to introduce myself.

Exercise 16. Using prepositions in idioms, p. 19

1. Children are waiting longer to become independent of their parents.

2. According to US Census data for young adults ages eighteen to twenty-four, 57 percent of men and 47 percent of women live full-time with their parents.

3. Some of these adult children are dependent on their parents financially.

4. In other cases, the parents charge their children for housing, food, and other living expenses.

5. Many adult children are financially capable of living independently but prefer to save money rather than contend with high housing costs.

Exercise 17. Revising: Clichés, p. 20

Possible answers

1. Our reliance on foreign oil to support our many cars has peaked in recent years.

2. Vehicles that get low gas mileage are responsible for part of the increase.

3. In the future, we may have to make difficult choices, using public transportation or driving only fuel-efficient cars.

4. Both solutions are <u>easy to propose</u> but <u>difficult to implement</u>.

5. But <u>we must acknowledge</u> that we cannot <u>continue to deplete</u> the world's oil reserves.

II. GRAMMATICAL SENTENCES

Verbs

Exercise 18. Using irregular verbs, p. 22

1. The world population has <u>grown</u> by two-thirds of a billion people in less than a decade. [Past participle.]

2. Recently it <u>broke</u> the 6 billion mark. [Past tense.]

3. Experts have <u>drawn</u> pictures of a crowded future. [Past participle.]

4. They predict that the world population may have <u>slid</u> up to as much as 10 billion by the year 2050. [Past participle.]

5. Though the food supply <u>rose</u> in the last decade, the share to each person <u>fell</u>. [Both past tense.]

6. At the same time the water supply, which had actually <u>become</u> healthier in the twentieth century, <u>sank</u> in size and quality. [Past participle; past tense.]

7. The number of species on earth <u>shrank</u> by 20 percent. [Past tense.]

8. Changes in land use <u>ran</u> nomads and subsistence farmers off the land. [Past tense.]

9. Yet all has not been <u>lost</u>. [Past participle.]

10. Recently human beings have <u>begun</u> to heed these and other problems and to explore how technology can be <u>driven</u> to help the earth and all its populations. [Both past participles.]

Exercise 19. Combining helping verbs and main verbs (ESL), p. 23

1. A report from the Bureau of the Census has <u>confirmed</u> a widening gap between rich and poor.

2. As suspected, the percentage of people below the poverty level did <u>increase</u> over the last decade.

3. More than 17 percent of the population is <u>making</u> 5 percent of all the income.

4. About 1 percent of the population will <u>be</u> keeping [*or* will <u>keep</u>] an average of $500,000 apiece after taxes.

5. Sentence correct.

6. More than 80 percent of American families <u>will make</u> [*or* <u>may make</u>] less than $65,000 per family this year.

7. Fewer than 5 percent of families <u>could make</u> more than $110,000 per family.

8. At the same time that the gap is <u>widening</u>, many people are <u>working</u> longer hours.

9. Many workers once might have <u>changed</u> jobs to increase their pay.

10. Now these workers are <u>remaining</u> with the jobs they have.

Exercise 20. Revising: Verbs plus gerunds or infinitives (ESL), p. 24

1. A program called HELP Wanted tries to encourage citizens <u>to</u> take action on behalf of American competitiveness.

2. Officials working on this program hope <u>to improve</u> education for work.

3. Sentence correct.

4. American businesses find that some workers need <u>to learn</u> to read.

5. In fact, many US companies have their workers <u>attend</u> classes.

6. New York Life Insurance Company quit <u>processing</u> claims in the US because of illiteracy among workers.

7. Motorola requires applicants <u>to take</u> an exam in math.

8. In the next ten years the United States expects <u>to face</u> a shortage of 350,000 scientists.

9. Sentence correct.

10. Sentence correct.

Exercise 21. Revising: Verbs plus particles (ESL), p. 25

1. American movies treat everything from going out with [correct] someone to making up [correct] an ethnic identity, but few people <u>look into their significance.</u>

2. While some viewers stay away from [correct] topical films, others <u>turn up at the theater</u> simply because a movie has sparked debate.

3. Some movies attracted rowdy viewers, and the theaters had to <u>throw them out.</u>

4. Filmmakers have always been eager to point their influence out [correct; *or* <u>point out their influence</u>] to the public.

5. Everyone agrees that filmmakers will <u>keep on creating controversy,</u> if only because it can fill up [correct] theaters.

Exercise 22. Adjusting tense sequence: Past or past perfect tense, p. 26

1. Diaries that Adolf Hitler <u>was supposed</u> to have written <u>had surfaced</u> in Germany.

2. Many people <u>believed</u> that the diaries <u>were</u> authentic because a well-known historian <u>had declared</u> them so.

3. However, the historian's evaluation <u>was questioned</u> by other authorities, who <u>called</u> the diaries forgeries.

4. They <u>claimed</u>, among other things, that the paper <u>was</u> not old enough to have <u>been</u> used by Hitler.

5. Eventually, the doubters <u>won</u> the debate because they <u>had</u> the best evidence.

Exercise 23. Revising: Consistency in tense and mood, p. 27

1. When your cholesterol count is too high, adjusting your diet and exercise level <u>reduces</u> it.

2. After you <u>lower</u> your cholesterol rate, you decrease the chances of heart attack and stroke.

3. First eliminate saturated fats from your diet; then <u>consume</u> more whole grains and raw vegetables.

4. To avoid saturated fats, substitute turkey and chicken for beef, and <u>use</u> cholesterol-free margarine, salad dressing, and cooking oil.

5. A regular program of aerobic exercise, such as walking or swimming, improves your cholesterol rate and <u>makes</u> you feel much healthier.

Exercise 24. Revising: Subjunctive mood, p. 28

1. If John Hawkins <u>had known</u> of all the dangerous side effects of smoking tobacco, would he have introduced the dried plant to England in 1565?

2. Hawkins noted that if a Florida Indian man <u>were</u> to travel for several days, he <u>would smoke</u> tobacco to satisfy his hunger and thirst.

3. Early tobacco growers feared that their product would not gain acceptance unless it <u>were</u> perceived as healthful.

4. To prevent fires, in 1646 the General Court of Massachusetts passed a law requiring that colonists <u>smoke</u> tobacco only if they were five miles from any town.

5. To prevent decadence, in 1647 Connecticut passed a law mandating that one's smoking of tobacco <u>be</u> limited to once a day in one's own home.

Exercise 25. Converting between active and passive voices, p. 29

1. When <u>engineers</u> <u>built</u> the Eiffel Tower in 1889, the <u>French</u> <u>thought</u> it to be ugly.

2. At the time, industrial <u>technology</u> <u>was</u> still <u>resisted</u> <u>by</u> many people.

3. The <u>technology</u> <u>was</u> <u>typified</u> <u>by</u> the tower's naked steel construction.

4. <u>People</u> <u>expected</u> beautiful ornament to grace fine buildings.

5. Further, <u>people</u> <u>could</u> <u>not</u> even <u>call</u> a structure without solid walls a building.

Exercise 26. Revising: Consistency in subject and voice, p. 30

1. If students learn how to study efficiently, <u>they will make</u> much better grades on tests.

2. Conscientious students begin to prepare for tests immediately after <u>they attend</u> the first class.

3. Before each class <u>the students complete</u> all reading assignments and answer any study questions.

4. In class they listen carefully and <u>take</u> good notes.

5. The students <u>ask questions</u> when they do not understand the instructor.

Exercise 27. Revising: Subject-verb agreement, p. 31

1. Weinstein & Associates <u>is</u> a consulting firm that <u>tries</u> to make businesspeople laugh.

2. Statistics from recent research <u>suggest</u> that humor relieves stress.

3. Reduced stress in businesses in turn <u>reduces</u> illness and absenteeism.

4. Reduced stress can also reduce friction within an employee group, which then <u>works</u> together more productively.

5. In special conferences held by one consultant, each of the participants <u>practices</u> making others laugh.

6. "Aren't there enough laughs within you to spread the wealth?" the consultant asks his students.

7. Sentence correct.

8. Such self-deprecating comments in public <u>are</u> uncommon among business managers, the consultant says.

9. Each of the managers in a typical firm <u>takes</u> the work much too seriously.

10. The humorous boss often feels like the only one of the managers who <u>has</u> other things in mind besides profits.

11. One consultant to many companies <u>suggests</u> cultivating office humor with practical jokes such as a rubber fish in the water cooler.

12. When a manager or employees regularly <u>post</u> cartoons on the bulletin board, office spirit usually picks up.

13. Sentence correct.

14. In the face of levity, the former sourpuss becomes one of those who <u>hide</u> bad temper.

15. Every one of the consultants <u>cautions</u>, however, that humor has no place in life-affecting corporate situations such as employee layoffs.

Pronouns

Exercise 28. Choosing subjective or objective pronouns, p. 33

1.	I	6.	her, me
2.	she, I, we	7.	her, me
3.	her, me	8.	she, I
4.	she, I, we	9.	I, we
5.	us, we	10.	her, me

Exercise 29. Choosing between *who* and *whom*, p. 34

1. whom	6. whom
2. who	7. who
3. whoever	8. whomever
4. Who	9. who
5. Whom	10. whom

Exercise 30. Revising: Pronoun forms, p. 35

1. Sentence correct.

2. Sentence correct.

3. He and Gilgamesh wrestled to see who was more powerful.

4. Sentence correct.

5. The friendship of the two strong men was sealed by their fighting.

6. Gilgamesh said, "Between you and me, mighty deeds will be accomplished, and our fame will be everlasting."

7. Among their glorious acts, Enkidu and he defeated a giant bull, Humbaba, and cut down the bull's cedar forests.

8. Sentence correct.

9. When Enkidu died, Gilgamesh mourned his death, realizing that no one had been a better friend than he.

10. When Gilgamesh himself died many years later, his people raised a monument praising Enkidu and him for their friendship and their mighty deeds of courage.

Exercise 31. Revising: Pronoun-antecedent agreement, p. 37

1. Each girl raised in a Mexican American family in the Rio Grande Valley of Texas hopes that one day she will be given a *quinceañera* party for her fifteenth birthday.

2. Such a celebration is very expensive because it entails a religious service followed by a huge party. *Or:* Such celebrations are very expensive because they entail a religious service followed by a huge party.

3. A girl's immediate family, unless it is wealthy, cannot afford the party
   by itself.

4. The parents will ask each close friend or relative if he or she can help
   with the preparations. *Or:* The parents will ask close friends or rela-
   tives if they can help with the preparations.

5. Sentence correct.

Exercise 32. Revising: Unclear pronoun reference, p. 38

Possible answers

1. There is a difference between the heroes of the twentieth century
   and the heroes of earlier times: twentieth-century heroes have flaws
   in their characters.

2. Sports fans still admire Pete Rose, Babe Ruth, and Joe Namath even
   though none of these heroes could be perfect.

3. Fans liked Rose for having his young son serve as bat boy when Rose
   was in Cincinnati.

4. Rose's reputation as a gambler and tax evader may overshadow his
   reputation as a ballplayer, but the latter will survive.

5. Rose amassed an unequaled record as a hitter, using his bat to do
   things no one else has ever done. The record stands even though Rose
   was banned from baseball.

6. Babe Ruth's drinking and carousing did not stop fans from cheering
   him.

7. Fans were happy if Ruth hit home runs and won games, and the Yankee
   owners wanted to fill the stadium. "The Bambino" seldom failed to satisfy the fans or the owners [*or* both the fans and the owners].

8. With his bat Ruth achieved the record for most home runs in a career.
   Nearly half a century passed before Henry Aaron broke the record.

9. When he was quarterback of the New York Jets, <u>Joe Namath</u> <u>told a</u> reporter, "<u>I will</u> have to quit because <u>I am</u> part-owner of a restaurant that mobsters supposedly also <u>own</u>."

10. Choosing between restaurant and career, Namath sold <u>the restaurant</u>.

Exercise 33. Revising: Specific antecedents, p. 40

Possible answers

1. "Life begins at forty" is a cliché many people live by, and this <u>saying</u> may or may not be true.

2. When <u>Pearl Buck</u> was forty, <u>her</u> novel *The Good Earth* won the Pulitzer Prize.

3. In *The Good Earth* <u>the characters</u> have to struggle, but fortitude is rewarded.

4. <u>The members of the British House of Commons</u> did not welcome forty-year-old Nancy Astor as the first female member when she entered in 1919.

5. In AD 610 Muhammad, age forty, began to have a series of visions that became the foundation of the Muslim faith. Since then, millions of people have become <u>Muslims</u>.

Exercise 34. Revising: Consistency in pronouns and antecedents, p. 41

1. When a taxpayer is waiting to receive a tax refund from the Internal Revenue Service, <u>he or she begins</u> to notice what time the mail carrier arrives. *Or:* When <u>taxpayers are</u> waiting to receive <u>tax refunds, they</u> begin to notice what time the mail carrier arrives.

2. If the taxpayer does not receive a refund check within six weeks of filing a return, <u>he or she</u> may not have followed the rules of the IRS. *Or:* If <u>taxpayers do</u> not receive <u>refund checks</u> within six weeks of filing a return, they may not have <u>followed the rules of the IRS.</u>

3. If <u>taxpayers</u> do not include <u>their</u> Social Security <u>numbers</u> on <u>returns, they</u> will have to wait for <u>refunds</u>. *Or:* A taxpayer who does not include <u>his or</u> <u>her</u> Social Security number on a return will have to wait for a refund.

4. When taxpayers do not file their <u>returns</u> early, they will not get <u>refunds</u> quickly.

5. If one has made errors on the tax form, <u>one</u> might even be audited, thereby delaying a refund even longer. *Or:* If one has made errors on the tax form, <u>he or she</u> might even be audited, thereby delaying a refund even longer.

Modifiers

Exercise 35. Revising: Adjectives and adverbs, p. 42

1. The eighteenth-century essayist Samuel Johnson fared <u>badly</u> in his early life.

2. Sentence correct.

3. After failing as a schoolmaster, Johnson moved to London, where he did <u>well</u>.

4. Johnson was taken <u>seriously</u> as a critic and dictionary maker.

5. Johnson was <u>really</u> surprised when he received a pension from King George III.

Exercise 36. Revising: Comparatives and superlatives, p. 43

1. The Brontë sisters are considered some of the <u>best</u> writers of their period.

2. Some readers think Emily Brontë's *Wuthering Heights* is the <u>saddest</u> novel they have ever read.

3. Many critics praise Emily more than <u>they do</u> the other two sisters, Charlotte and Anne. [*Also possible but improbable:* Many critics praise Emily more than the other two sisters, Charlotte and Anne, <u>did</u>.]

4. Critics still argue about whether Charlotte or Emily wrote <u>better</u>.

5. Certainly this family of women novelists was <u>unique</u>.

Exercise 37. Revising: Present and past participles (ESL), p. 44

1. Several critics found Alice Walker's *The Color Purple* to be a <u>fascinating</u> book.

2. Sentence correct.

3. Another critic argued that although the book contained many <u>depressing</u> episodes, the overall effect was <u>exciting</u>.

4. Since other readers found the book <u>annoying</u>, this critic pointed out its many surprising [correct] qualities.

5. In the end most critics agreed that the book was a <u>satisfying</u> novel about the struggles of an African American woman.

Exercise 38. Revising: Articles (ESL), p. 45

From <u>the</u> native American Indians who migrated from Asia 20,000 years ago to <u>the</u> new arrivals who now come by planes, <u>the</u> United States is a nation of foreigners. It is <u>a</u> country of immigrants who are all living under a single flag.
Back in <u>the</u> seventeenth and eighteenth centuries, at least 75 percent of the population came from England. However, between 1820 and 1975 more than 38 million immigrants came to this country from elsewhere in Europe. Many children of <u>the</u> immigrants were self-conscious and denied their heritage; many even refused to learn <u>the</u> native language of their parents and grandparents. They tried to "Americanize" themselves. The so-called Melting Pot theory of social change stressed <u>the</u> importance of blending everyone together into <u>a</u> kind of stew. Each nationality would contribute its own flavor, but <u>the</u> final stew would be something called "American."
This Melting Pot theory was never completely successful. In the last half of the twentieth century, <u>an</u> ethnic revival changed <u>the</u> metaphor. Many people now see American society as a mosaic. Americans are once again proud of their heritage, and ethnic differences make <u>the</u> mosaic colorful and interesting.

Exercise 39. Revising: Misplaced modifiers, p. 46

1. Women have contributed much <u>of great value</u> to American culture.

2. For example, <u>during the colonial era</u> Elizabeth Pinckney introduced indigo, the source of a valuable blue dye.

3. In 1821 Emma Willard founded the Troy Female Seminary, the first institution to provide a college-level education for women.

4. Mary Lyon founded Mount Holyoke Female Seminary as the first true women's college with a campus and directors who would sustain the college even after Lyon's death.

5. *Una*, which was founded by Pauline Wright Davis in 1853, was the first US newspaper that was dedicated to gaining women's rights.

6. Mitchell's Comet, which was named for Maria Mitchell, was discovered in 1847.

7. Mitchell, who lived from 1818 to 1889, was the first American woman astronomer.

8. She was a member of the first faculty at Vassar College.

9. When elected to the American Academy of Arts and Sciences in 1848, she was the first woman to join the prestigious organization.

10. When asked about her many accomplishments, Mitchell said that she was persistent rather than especially capable.

Exercise 40. Revising: Dangling modifiers, p. 47

Possible answers

1. After Andrew Jackson had accomplished many deeds of valor, his fame led to his election to the presidency in 1828 and 1832.

2. When Jackson was fourteen, both of his parents died.

3. To aid the American Revolution, Jackson chose service as a mounted courier.

4. Sentence correct.

5. Though not well educated, Jackson proved his ability in a successful career as a lawyer and judge.

6. Because Jackson won many military battles, the American public believed in his leadership.

7. Earning the nicknames "Old Hickory" and "Sharp Knife," Jackson established his military prowess in the War of 1812.

8. Losing only six dead and ten wounded, the triumphant Battle of New Orleans burnished Jackson's reputation.

9. Jackson's victories over raiding parties from Florida helped pressure Spain to cede that territory.

10. While briefly governor of Florida, Jackson set the US presidency as his goal.

Sentence Faults

Exercise 41. Identifying and revising sentence fragments, p. 49

Possible answers

1. Lacks a subject and a verb.
   Complete: An article about vandalism against works of art was interesting.
   Combined: In an interesting article about vandalism against works of art, the author says the vandals' motives vary widely.

2. Lacks a verb.
   Complete: The motives of the vandals vary widely.
   Combined: The motives of the vandals varying widely, researchers can make few generalizations.

3. Complete sentence.

4. Lacks a subject and a verb.
   Complete: But the vandal is not necessarily angry at the artist or the owner.
   Combined: Whoever harms artwork is usually angry, but not necessarily at the artist or the owner.

5. Lacks a verb for the subject <u>man</u>.
   Complete: For instance, <u>a man hammered at</u> Michelangelo's *Pietà*.
   Combined: For instance, a man who hammered at Michelangelo's *Pietà* <u>was angry at the Roman Catholic Church.</u>

6. Lacks a subject.
   Complete: <u>He</u> knocked off the Virgin Mary's nose.
   Combined: <u>A man hammered at Michelangelo's *Pietà* and knocked off the Virgin Mary's nose.</u>

7. Begins with subordinating conjunction.
   Complete: He was angry at the Roman Catholic Church.
   Combined: <u>A man hammered at Michelangelo's *Pietà*</u> because he was angry at the Roman Catholic Church.

8. Begins with *which* but is not a question.
   Complete: <u>The Church</u> knew nothing of his grievance.
   Combined: <u>He was angry at the Roman Catholic Church</u>, which knew nothing of his grievance.

9. Begins with subordinating conjunction.
   Complete: Many damaged works can be repaired.
   Combined: Although many damaged works can be repaired, <u>even the most skillful repairs are forever visible.</u>

10. Complete sentence.

Exercise 42. Revising: Sentence fragments, p. 50

Possible revision

People generally avoid eating mushrooms except those they buy in stores. But in fact many varieties of mushrooms are edible. Mushrooms are members of a large group of vegetation called nonflowering plants, <u>includ</u>ing algae, mosses, ferns and coniferous trees, <u>even the giant redwoods of California. Most of the nonflowering plants prefer moist environments such</u> as forest floors, fallen timber, and still water. Mushrooms, for example, <u>pre</u>fer moist, shady soil. Algae grow in water.

Most mushrooms, both edible and inedible, are members of a class called basidium fungi, a term referring to their method of reproduction. The basidia produce spores, which can develop into mushrooms. This classification includes the prized meadow mushroom, cultivated commercially, and the amanitas. The amanita group contains both edible and poisonous species. Another familiar group of mushrooms, the puffballs, are easily identified by their round shape. Their spores are contained under a thick skin, which eventually ruptures to release the spores. The famous morels are in still another group. These pitted, spongy mushrooms are called sac fungi because the spores develop in sacs.

Anyone interested in mushrooms as food should heed the US Public Health Service warning not to eat any wild mushrooms unless their identity and edibility are established without a doubt.

Exercise 43. Revising: Comma splices and fused sentences, p. 52

Possible answers

1. Money has a long history. It goes back at least as far as the earliest records.

   Money has a long history; it goes back at least as far as the earliest records.

2. Many of the earliest records concern financial transactions; indeed, early history must often be inferred from commercial activity.

   Many of the earliest records concern financial transactions. Indeed, early history must often be inferred from commercial activity.

3. Sentence correct.

4. Although sometimes the objects have had real value, in modern times their value has been more abstract.

   Sometimes the objects have had real value; however, in modern times their value has been more abstract.

5. Cattle, fermented beverages, and rare shells have served as money, and each one had actual value for the society.

   Cattle, fermented beverages, and rare shells have served as money. Each one had actual value for the society.

6. As money, these objects acquired additional value <u>because</u> they represented other goods.

   As money, these objects acquired additional value<u>;</u> they represented other goods.

7. Today money may be made of worthless paper<u>, or</u> it may even consist of a bit of data in a computer's memory.

   Today money may be made of worthless paper. <u>It</u> may even consist of a bit of data in a computer's memory.

8. We think of money as valuable<u>, but</u> only our common faith in it makes it valuable.

   <u>Although</u> we think of money as valuable<u>,</u> only our common faith in it makes it valuable.

9. That faith is sometimes fragile<u>;</u> consequently, currencies themselves are fragile.

   That faith is sometimes fragile. <u>C</u>onsequently, currencies themselves are fragile.

10. Economic crises often shake the belief in money<u>;</u> indeed, such weakened faith helped cause the Great Depression of the 1930s.

    Economic crises often shake the belief in money. <u>I</u>ndeed, such weakened faith helped cause the Great Depression of the 1930s.

11. Throughout history money and religion were closely linked<u>, for</u> there was little distinction between government and religion.

    Throughout history money and religion were closely linked <u>because</u> there was little distinction between government and religion.

12. Sentence correct.

13. These powerful leaders decided what objects would serve as money<u>, and</u> their backing encouraged public faith in the money.

    These powerful leaders decided what objects would serve as money<u>.</u> <u>T</u>heir backing encouraged public faith in the money.

14. If coins were minted of precious metals, the religious overtones of money were then strengthened.

    Coins were minted of precious metals; the religious overtones of money were then strengthened.

15. Because people already believed the precious metals to be divine, their use in money intensified its allure.

    People already believed the precious metals to be divine; thus their use in money intensified its allure.

Exercise 44. Revising: Comma splices and fused sentences, p. 54

Possible revision

All those parents who urged their children to eat broccoli were right, for the vegetable really is healthful. Broccoli contains sulforaphane; moreover, this mustard oil can be found in kale and Brussels sprouts. Sulforaphane causes the body to make an enzyme that attacks carcinogens, which cause cancer. The enzyme speeds up the work of the kidneys, and then they can flush harmful chemicals out of the body. Other vegetables have similar benefits; however, green, leafy vegetables like broccoli are the most efficient. Thus, wise people will eat their broccoli. It could save their lives.

III. PUNCTUATION

Exercise 45. Using the comma between linked main clauses, p. 56

1. Parents once automatically gave their children the father's last name, but some no longer do.

2. Parents may now give their children any last name they choose, and the arguments for choosing the mother's last name are often strong and convincing.

3. The child's last name may be just the mother's, or it may link the mother's and the father's with a hyphen.

4. Sometimes the first and third children will have the mother's last name, and the second child will have the father's.

5. Occasionally, the mother and father combine parts of their names, and a new last name is formed.

Exercise 46. Using the comma with introductory elements, p. 57

1. Veering sharply to the right, a large flock of birds neatly avoids a high wall.

2. Sentence correct.

3. With the help of complex computer simulations, zoologists are learning more about this movement.

4. As it turns out, evading danger is really an individual response.

5. Multiplied over hundreds of individuals, these responses look as if they have been choreographed.

Exercise 47. Punctuating essential and nonessential elements, p. 57

1. Italians insist that Marco Polo, the thirteenth-century explorer, did not import pasta from China.

2. Pasta, which consists of flour and water and often egg, existed in Italy long before Marco Polo left for his travels.

3. Sentence correct.

4. Most Italians dispute this account, although their evidence is shaky.

5. Wherever it originated, the Italians are now the undisputed masters in making and cooking pasta.

6. Sentence correct.

7. Most cooks buy dried pasta, lacking the time to make their own.

8. Sentence correct.

9. Pasta manufacturers choose hard durum wheat because it makes firmer cooked pasta than common wheat does.

10. Pasta made from common wheat gets soggy in boiling water.

Exercise 48. Using the comma with series and adjectives, p. 58

1. Shoes with high heels were originally designed to protect feet from mud, garbage, and animal waste in the streets.

2. Sentence correct.

3. The heels were worn by men and made of colorful silk fabrics, soft suedes, or smooth leathers.

4. High-heeled shoes became popular when the short, powerful King Louis XIV of France began wearing them.

5. Louis's influence was so strong that men and women of the court, priests and cardinals, and even household servants wore high heels.

Exercise 49. Using the comma with quotations, p. 59

1. Sentence correct.

2. "I think of the open-ended writing process as a voyage in two stages," Elbow says.

3. "The sea voyage is a process of divergence, branching, proliferation, and confusion," Elbow continues; "the coming to land is a process of convergence, pruning, centralizing, and clarifying."

4. "Keep up one session of writing long enough to get loosened up and tired," advises Elbow, "long enough in fact to make a bit of a voyage."

5. "In coming to new land," Elbow says, "you develop a new conception of what you are writing about."

Exercise 50. Revising: Needless and misused commas, p. 60

1. Nearly 32 million US residents speak a first language other than English.

2. After English the languages most commonly spoken in the United States are Spanish, French, and German.

3. Almost 75 percent of the people who speak foreign languages used the words "good" or "very good" when judging their proficiency in English.

4. Sentence correct.

5. The states with the highest proportion of foreign-language speakers are New Mexico and California.

Exercise 51. Revising: Commas, p. 61

Ellis Island, New York, reopened for business in 1990, but now the customers are tourists, not immigrants. This spot, which lies in New York Harbor, was the first American soil seen or touched by many of the nation's immigrants. Though other places also served as ports of entry for foreigners, none has the symbolic power of Ellis Island. Between its opening in 1892 and its closing in 1954, over 20 million people, about two-thirds of all immigrants, were detained there before taking up their new lives in the United States. Ellis Island processed over 2000 [*or* 2,000] newcomers a day when immigration was at its peak between 1900 and 1920.

As the end of a long voyage and the introduction to the New World, Ellis Island must have left something to be desired. The "huddled masses," as the Statue of Liberty calls them, indeed were huddled. New arrivals were herded about, kept standing in lines for hours or days, yelled at, and abused. Assigned numbers, they submitted their bodies to the pokings and proddings of the silent nurses and doctors who were charged with ferreting out the slightest sign of sickness, disability, or insanity. That test having been passed, the immigrants faced interrogation by an official through an interpreter. Those with names deemed inconveniently long or difficult to pronounce often found themselves permanently labeled with abbreviations of their names or with the names of their hometowns. But millions survived the examination, humiliation, and confusion to take the last short boat ride to New York City. For many of them and especially for their descendants, Ellis Island eventually became not a nightmare, but the place where a new life began.

Exercise 52. Using the semicolon between main clauses, p. 62

1. Computers can process any information that can be represented numerically; consequently, they can process musical information.

2. A computer's ability to process music depends on what software it can run; furthermore, it must be connected to a system that converts electrical vibration into sound.

3. Computers and their sound systems can produce many different sounds; in fact, the number of possible sounds is infinite.

4. Musicians have always experimented with new technology; audiences have always resisted the experiments.

5. The computer is not the first new technology in music; indeed, the pipe organ and saxophone were also technological breakthroughs in their day.

6. Most computer musicians are not merely following the latest fad; they are discovering new sounds and new ways to manipulate sound.

7. More and more musicians are playing computerized instruments; more and more listeners are worrying about the future of acoustic instruments.

8. Few musicians have abandoned acoustic instruments; most value acoustic sounds as much as electronic sounds.

9. The powerful music computers are very expensive; they are therefore used only by professional musicians. *Or:* . . . they are, therefore, used only by professional musicians.

10. These music computers are too expensive for the average consumer; however, digital keyboards can be less expensive and are widely available.

Exercise 53. Revising: Semicolons, p. 64

The set, sounds, and actors in the movie captured the essence of horror films. The set was ideal: dark, deserted streets; trees dipping their branches over the sidewalks; mist hugging the ground and creeping up to meet the trees; looming shadows of unlighted, turreted houses. The sounds, too, were appropriate; especially terrifying was the hard, hollow sound of footsteps echoing throughout the film. But the best feature of the movie was its actors, all of them tall, pale, and thin to the point of emaciation. With one exception, they were dressed uniformly in gray and had gray hair. The exception was an actress who dressed only in black, as if to set off her pale yellow, nearly white, long hair, the only color in the film. The glinting black eyes of another actor stole almost every scene; indeed, they were the source of the film's mischief.

Exercise 54. Revising: Colons and semicolons, p. 65

1. Sunlight is made up of three kinds of radiation: visible rays; infrared rays, which we cannot see; and ultraviolet rays, which are also invisible.

2. Especially in the ultraviolet range, sunlight is harmful to the eyes.

3. Ultraviolet rays can damage the retina; furthermore, they can cause cataracts on the lens.

4. Infrared rays are the longest, measuring 700 nanometers and longer, while ultraviolet rays are the shortest, measuring 400 nanometers and shorter.

5. The lens protects the eye by absorbing much of the ultraviolet radiation and thus shielding the retina.

6. By protecting the retina, however, the lens becomes a victim, growing cloudy and blocking vision.

7. The best way to protect your eyes is to wear hats that shade the face and sunglasses that screen out the ultraviolet rays.

8. Sentence correct.

9. Sunglasses should screen out ultraviolet rays and be dark enough so that people can't see your eyes through them; otherwise, the lenses will not protect your eyes, and you will be at risk for cataracts later in life.

10. People who spend much time outside in the sun really owe it to themselves to buy a pair of sunglasses that will shield their eyes.

Exercise 55. Revising: Apostrophes, p. 66

People whose online experiences include blogging, Web cams, and social-networking sites are often used to seeing the details of other people's private lives. Many are also comfortable sharing their own opinions, photographs, and videos with family, friends, and even strangers. However, they need to realize that employers and even the government can see <u>their</u> information, too. Employers commonly put <u>applicants'</u> names through social-networking Web sites such as *MySpace* and *Facebook*. Many companies monitor their <u>employees'</u> outbound e-mail. People can take steps to protect their personal information by adjusting the privacy settings on their social-networking pages. [Sentence correct.] They can avoid posting photos of themselves that they <u>wouldn't</u> want an employer to see. They can avoid sending personal e-mail while <u>they're</u> at work. <u>It's</u> the <u>individual's</u> responsibility to keep certain information private.

Exercise 56. Revising: Quotation marks, p. 67

In one class we talked about a passage from "I Have a Dream," the speech delivered by Martin Luther King, Jr., on the steps of the Lincoln Memorial on August 28, 1963:

> When the architects of our republic wrote the magnificent words of the Constitution and the Declaration of Independence, they were signing a promissory note to which every American was to fall heir. This note was a promise that all men would be guaranteed the unalienable rights of life, liberty, and the pursuit of happiness.

"What did Dr. King mean by this statement?" the teacher asked. "Perhaps we should define 'promissory note' first." Then she explained that a person who signs such a note agrees to pay a specific sum of money on a particular date or on demand by the holder of the note.

One student suggested, "Maybe Dr. King meant that the writers of the Constitution and Declaration promised that all people in America should be equal."

"He and over 200,000 people had gathered in Washington, DC," added another student. "Maybe their purpose was to demand payment, to demand those rights for African Americans."

The whole discussion was an eye-opener for those of us (including me) who had never considered that those documents make promises that we should expect our country to fulfill.

Exercise 57. Revising: End punctuation, p. 68

When visitors first arrive in Hawaii, they often encounter an unexpected language barrier. Standard English is the language of business and government, but many of the people speak Pidgin English. Instead of an excited "Aloha!" the visitors may be greeted with an excited Pidgin "Howzit!" or asked if they know "how fo' find one good hotel." Many Hawaiians question whether Pidgin will hold children back because it prevents communication with *haoles*, or Caucasians, who run businesses. Yet many others feel that Pidgin is a last defense of ethnic diversity on the islands. To those who want to make standard English the official language of the state, these Hawaiians may respond, "Just 'cause I speak Pidgin no mean I dumb." They may ask, "Why you no listen?" or, in standard English, "Why don't you listen?"

Exercise 58. Using ellipsis marks, p. 69

1. "To be able to read the Bible in the vernacular was a liberating experience. . . ."

2. "To be able to read the Bible in the vernacular . . . freed the reader from hearing only the set passages read in the church and interpreted by the church."

3. "Women in the sixteenth and seventeenth centuries were educated in the home and, in some cases, in boarding schools. . . . A Protestant woman was expected to read the scriptures daily, to meditate on them, and to memorize portions of them."

Exercise 59. Revising: Punctuation, p. 70

Brewed coffee is the most widely consumed beverage in the world. The trade in coffee beans alone amounts to well over $6,000,000,000 a year, and the total volume of beans traded exceeds 4,250,000 tons a year. It's believed that the beverage was introduced into Arabia in the fifteenth century AD [correct; *or* A.D.], probably by Ethiopians. By the middle or late sixteenth century, the Arabs had introduced the beverage to the Europeans, who at first resisted it because of its strong flavor and effect as a mild stimulant. The French, Italians, and other Europeans incorporated coffee into their diets by the seventeenth century; the English, however, preferred tea, which they were then importing from India. Since America was colonized primarily by the English, Americans also preferred tea. Only after the Boston Tea Party (1773) did Americans begin drinking coffee in large quantities. Now, though, the US [correct; *or* U.S.] is one of the top coffee-consuming countries, consumption having been spurred on by familiar advertising claims: "Good till the last drop"; "Rich, hearty aroma"; "Always rich, never bitter."

Produced from the fruit of an evergreen tree, coffee is grown primarily in Latin America, southern Asia, and Africa. Coffee trees require a hot climate, high humidity, rich soil with good drainage, and partial shade; consequently, they thrive on the east or west slopes of tropical volcanic mountains, where the soil is laced with potash and drains easily. The coffee beans—actually seeds—grow inside bright red berries. The berries are picked by hand, and the beans are extracted by machine, leaving a pulpy fruit residue that can be used for fertilizer. The beans are usually roasted in ovens, a chemical process that releases the beans' essential oil (caffeol), which gives coffee its distinctive aroma. Over a hundred different varieties of beans are produced in the world, each with a different flavor attributable to three factors: the species of plant (*Coffea arabia* and *Coffea robusta* are the most common) and the soil and climate where the variety was grown.

IV. SPELLING AND MECHANICS

Exercise 60. Using correct spellings, p. 72

1. Science <u>affects</u> many <u>important</u> aspects of our lives.

2. Many people have a <u>poor</u> understanding of the <u>role</u> of scientific breakthroughs in <u>their</u> health.

3. Many people <u>believe</u> that <u>doctors</u> are more <u>responsible</u> for <u>improvements</u> in health care than scientists are.

4. But scientists in the <u>laboratory</u> have made crucial steps in the search for <u>knowledge</u> about health and <u>medicine</u>.

5. For example, one scientist <u>whose</u> discoveries have <u>affected</u> many people is Ulf Von Euler.

6. In the 1950s Von Euler's discovery of certain hormones <u>led</u> to the invention of the birth control pill.

7. Von Euler's work was used by John Rock, who <u>developed</u> the first birth control pill and influenced family <u>planning</u>.

8. Von Euler also discovered the <u>principal</u> neurotransmitter that controls the heartbeat.

9. Another scientist, Hans Selye, showed what <u>effect</u> stress can have on the body.

10. His findings have <u>led</u> to methods of <u>bearing</u> stress.

Exercise 61. Revising: Hyphens, p. 73

1. Sentence correct.

2. Sentence correct.

3. The non-African elephants of south-central Asia are somewhat smaller.

4. A fourteen- or fifteen-year-old elephant has reached sexual maturity.

5. The elephant life span is about sixty-five or seventy years.

6. Sentence correct.

7. It stands about thirty-three inches high.

8. A two-hundred-pound, thirty-three-inch baby is quite a big baby.

9. Unfortunately, elephants are often killed for their ivory tusks, and partly as a result they are an increasingly endangered species.

10. Sentence correct.

Exercise 62. Revising: Capital letters, p. 74

1. San Antonio, Texas, is a thriving city in the Southwest.

2. The city has always offered much to tourists interested in the roots of Spanish settlement of the New World.

3. The Alamo is one of five Catholic missions built by priests to convert Native Americans and to maintain Spain's claims in the area.

4. But the Alamo is more famous for being the site of an 1836 battle that helped to create the Republic of Texas.

5. Many of the nearby streets, such as Crockett Street, are named for men who died in that battle.

6. The Hemisfair Plaza and the San Antonio River link tourist and convention facilities.

7. Restaurants, hotels, and shops line the river. The haunting melodies of "Una Paloma Blanca" and "Malagueña" lure passing tourists into Casa Rio and other Mexican restaurants.

8. The University of Texas at San Antonio has expanded, and a medical center lies in the northwest part of the city.

9. Sentence correct.

10. The city has attracted high-tech industry, creating a corridor between San Antonio and Austin.

Exercise 63. Revising: Italics or underlining, p. 75

1. Of the many Vietnam veterans who are writers, Oliver Stone is perhaps the most famous for writing and directing the films (*Platoon*) and (*Born on the Fourth of July*).

2. Tim O'Brien has written short stories for (*Esquire*), (*GQ*), and (*Massachusetts Review*).

3. (*Going After Cacciato*) is O'Brien's dreamlike novel about the horrors of combat.

4. The word (*Vietnam*) is technically two words (*Viet* and *Nam*), but most American writers spell it as (one) word. [*Viet* and *Nam* were correctly highlighted. Highlighting removed from *one*.]

5. American writers use words or phrases borrowed from Vietnamese, such as (*di di mau*) ("go quickly") or (*dinky dau*) ("crazy").

6. Philip Caputo's (gripping) account of his service in Vietnam appears in the book (*A Rumor of War*). [Highlighting removed from *gripping*.]

7. Sentence correct.

8. David Rabe's plays—including (*The Basic Training of Pavlo Hummel, Streamers*), and (*Sticks and Bones*)—depict the effects of the war (not only) on the soldiers (but also) on their families. [Highlighting removed from *not only . . . but also*.]

9. Called the (poet laureate of the Vietnam war), Steve Mason has published two collections of poems: (*Johnny's Song*) and (*Warrior for Peace*). [Highlighting removed from *poet laureate of the Vietnam war*.]

10. (*The Washington Post*) published (rave) reviews of (*Veteran's Day*), an autobiography by Rod Kane. [Highlighting removed from *rave*.]

Exercise 64. Revising: Abbreviations, p. 77

1. Sentence correct.

2. About 65 <u>million</u> <u>years</u> ago, a comet or asteroid crashed into the earth.

3. The result was a huge crater about 10 <u>kilometers</u> (6.2 <u>miles</u>) deep in the Gulf of <u>Mexico</u>.

4. Sharpton's new measurements suggest that the crater is 50 <u>percent</u> larger than scientists had previously believed.

5. Indeed, 20-<u>year</u>-old drilling cores reveal that the crater is about 186 <u>miles</u> wide, roughly the size of <u>Connecticut</u>.

6. Sentence correct.

7. On impact, 200,000 cubic <u>kilometers</u> of rock and soil were vaporized or thrown into the air.

8. That's the equivalent of 2.34 <u>billion</u> cubic <u>feet</u> of matter.

9. The impact would have created 400-<u>foot</u> tidal waves across the <u>Atlantic</u> <u>Ocean</u>, <u>temperatures</u> higher than 20,000 <u>degrees</u>, and powerful earthquakes.

10. Sharpton theorizes that the dust, vapor, and smoke from this impact blocked the sun's rays for <u>months</u>, cooled the earth, and thus resulted in the death of the dinosaurs.

Exercise 65. Revising: Numbers, p. 78

1. The planet Saturn is <u>900</u> million miles, or nearly <u>1.5 billion</u> kilometers, from the sun.

2. Sentence correct.

3. Thus, Saturn orbits the sun only <u>2.4</u> times during the average human life span.

4. It travels in its orbit at about <u>21,600</u> miles per hour.

5. <u>Fifteen</u> to <u>twenty</u> times denser than Earth's core, Saturn's core measures <u>seventeen thousand</u> miles across.

6. The temperature at Saturn's cloud tops is <u>−170</u> degrees Fahrenheit.

7. In <u>1933</u>, astronomers found on Saturn's surface a huge white spot <u>two</u> times the size of Earth and <u>seven</u> times the size of Mercury.

8. Saturn's famous rings reflect almost <u>70</u> percent of the sunlight that approaches the planet.

9. The ring system is almost <u>40,000</u> miles wide, beginning 8,800 miles from the planet's visible surface and ending <u>47,000</u> miles from that surface.

10. The spacecraft *Cassini* traveled more than <u>820 million</u> miles to explore and photograph Saturn.

V. RESEARCH AND DOCUMENTATION

Exercise 66. Synthesizing sources, p. 80

The key similarities and differences are these:

> *Similarities:* Nadelmann and Posey agree that crackdowns or penalties do not stop the drug trade. Nadelmann and Runkle agree that the drug trade affects the young, who are most impressionable.

> *Differences:* Nadelmann maintains that the illegal drug trade does more to entice youths to drugs than do the drugs themselves, whereas Runkle maintains that the illegality discourages youths from using prohibited drugs. Posey, in contrast to Runkle, claims that penalties do nothing to discourage drug abusers.

Students' paragraphs will depend on their views, but here is a sample response:

> Posey seems to invalidate the whole debate over drug legalization: nothing, he says from experience, will stop drug abuse. But such a futile view, whatever its truth, cannot stop the search for a solution. We have tried the prohibition favored by Runkle. Even if, as she claims, students are using fewer illegal drugs, prohibition has not worked. It may be time to try the admittedly risky approach proposed by Nadelmann, legalizing drugs to "drive the drug-dealing business off the streets."

Exercise 67. Summarizing and paraphrasing, p. 81

Possible summary

Federalism, unlike a unitary system, allows the states autonomy. Its strength and its weakness—which are in balance—lie in the regional differences it permits.

Possible paraphrase

Under federalism, each state can devise its own ways of handling problems and its own laws. The system's advantage is that a state can operate according to its people's culture, morals, and wealth. A unitary system like that in France does not permit such diversity.

Exercise 68. Combining summary, paraphrase, and direct quotation, p. 82

Possible answer

Speakers at parties often "unconsciously duel" in conversations in order to assert "dominance" over others. A speaker may mumble, thus preventing a listener from understanding what is said. Or he or she may continue talking after the listener has moved away, a "challenge to the listener to return and acknowledge the dominance of the speaker."

Exercise 69. Integrating sources, p. 83

Sample paragraph

Why does a woman who is otherwise happy regularly suffer anxiety attacks at the first sign of spring? Why does a man who is otherwise a competent, relaxed driver feel panic whenever he approaches a traffic rotary? According to Willard Gaylin, a professor of psychiatry and a practicing psychoanalyst, such feelings of anxiety are attributable to the uniquely human capacities for remembering, imagining, and forming "symbolic and often unconscious representations" of experiences (23). The feeling of anxiety, Gaylin says, "is . . . compounded by its seemingly irrational quality": it may appear despite the absence of an immediate source of worry or pain (23). The anxious woman is not aware of it, but her father's death twenty years before in April has caused her to equate spring with death. Similarly, the man has forgotten that a terrible accident he witnessed as a child occurred at a rotary. For both people, the anxious feelings are not reduced but heightened because they seem to be unfounded.

Exercise 70. Recognizing plagiarism, p. 83

1. Plagiarized: takes phrases directly from the original without quotation marks.

2. Acceptable: acknowledges the source, uses quotation marks around copied words, and uses brackets around an addition to the quotation.

3. Inaccurate and plagiarized: the passage uses phrases from the original without quotation marks and distorts its meaning.

4. Acceptable: acknowledges the source, restates the original in new words, and correctly conveys its meaning.

5. Inaccurate and plagiarized: fails to acknowledge the source and fails to convey accurately the concepts of "discrimination" and "confusing" outlined in the original.

6. Inaccurate: ellipses are needed to indicate that material was omitted, and brackets must be placed around lowercase *s* in society. In addition, the editing of the passage omits mention of "psychiatric labeling," the focus of the original.

Exercise 71. Writing works-cited entries, p. 85

The answers below are in MLA style and alphabetized.

Eggert, Wayne G. "State and Local Sales/Use Tax Simplification." *The Sales Tax in the Twenty-first Century.* Ed. Matthew N. Murray and William F. Fox. Westport: Praeger, 2004. 67-80. Print.

"The Internet Tax Freedom Act and the Digital Divide." *Center on Budget and Policy Priorities.* Center on Budget and Policy Priorities, 26 Sept. 2007. Web. 2 Apr. 2010.

James, Nora. E-mail interview. 1 Apr. 2010.

Novack, Janet. "Point, Click, Pay Tax." *Forbes* 28 Nov. 2007: 56-58. *Proquest.* Web. 10 Apr. 2010.

Osborne, Sally G. *All's Fair in Internet Commerce, or Is It?* New York: Random, 2004. Print.

United States. Advisory Commission on Electronic Commerce. *Report to Congress.* US Advisory Commission on Electronic Commerce, Apr. 2005. Web. 12 Apr. 2010.

Zimmerman, Malai, and Kent Hoover. "Use of Third Parties to Collect State and Local Taxes on Internet Sales." *Pacific Business Journal* 5.2 (2004): 45-48. Print.